Historic Landmarks of
Port of Spain

Michael Anthony
With a Foreword by Bridget Brereton
Edited by Anthony Luengo

MACMILLAN
CARIBBEAN

Macmillan Education Limited
Between Towns Road, Oxford OX4 3PP
A division of Macmillan Publishers Limited
Companies and representatives throughout the world

www.macmillan-caribbean.com

ISBN: 978-0-333-97555-8

Text © Michael Anthony 2008
Foreword © Bridget Brereton 2008
Design and illustration © Macmillan Publishers Limited 2008

All rights reserved; no part of this publication may be reproduced, stored in a retrieval system, transmitted in any form or by any means, electronic, mechanical, photocopying, recording or otherwise, without the prior written permission of the publishers.

Design by Bob Swan
Cover design by Gareth Jenkins at Above Studios, Trinidad
Maps by Peter Harper
Typeset by Carol Hulme

The authors and publishers would like to thank the following for permission to reproduce photographs their photographic material:

All cover photographs: Alex Smailes

Michael Anthony: p.iii, p.xiv, p4, p10(t), p10(b), p11, p14

Adrian Camps-Campins: p2(b), p3(tl), p3(b), p19(tr), p30(b), p31, p55, p62, p72(b)

The Illustrated London News: p27

The Library of Congress, Washington D.C.: p6,

Paria Publishing: p.xiii, p.xvii, p89

Alex Smailes: Title page illustrations, p.iv(bl), p.iv(tr), p.v(tl), p.v(bottom), p.vi, p2 (tl), p5, p7, p8, p9, p12, p13, p15, p17, p18, p19 (bottom), p20, p21, p22, p23, p24, p26, p28, p29, p30 (tr), p32, p33, p34, p35, p36, p37, p38, p39, p41, p42, p43, p44, p45, p46, p47, p48, p49(l), p49(r), p50, p51, p52, p53, p54, p56, p57, p58, p59, p60(bl), p60 (tr), p61, p63, p64, p65, p66, p67, p69, p70, p72(tr), p73, p74, p75, p76, p78(bl), p78(br), p79, p80, p81, p82, p83, p84, p85, p86, p87, p88

Bob Swan: p1

Printed and bound in Thailand

2012 2011 2010 2009 2008
10 9 8 7 6 5 4 3 2 1

Contents

Foreword vii

Map of Trinidad viii

Plans of Port of Spain ix

Introduction xii

1 Central Port of Spain (Independence Square, South Quay, and the Waterfront)

Independence Square and Brian Lara Promenade — 1

Fort San Andrés/City Museum of Port of Spain — 5

Cathedral of the Immaculate Conception — 6

The Port of Spain Lighthouse — 8

Columbus Square — 9

South Quay and the Waterfront — 9

Railway Headquarters Building/City Gate — 11

The Cipriani Statue — 13

The Treasury Building — 14

The Eric Williams Financial Complex — 15

Colonial Life Building — 17

2 Central Port of Spain (East)

United Brothers Masonic Lodge — 18

Fort Chacón — 19

Fort Picton — 20

L'Hospice of St Vincent de Paul — 21

The Drinking Trough — 22

3 Central Port of Spain (Woodford Square Area)

Woodford Square — 23

The Red House — 25

Trinity Cathedral — 28

Hall of Justice — 30

City Hall — 31

Old Library Building — 32

National Library — 33

Old Fire Brigade Building — 34

Greyfriars Church — 35

Old Police Headquarters — 36

Cabildo Building — 37

4 Central Port of Spain ('Uptown')

Globe Cinema	39
The Church of the Holy Rosary	40
St Joseph's Convent	42
St Mary's College	44
The Port of Spain State Prison	46
Port of Spain General Hospital	47
St Ann's Church of Scotland	48
Lapeyrouse Cemetery	49

5 Newtown

St Patrick's Church	50
Jenny's	51

6 Queen's Park Savannah Area (South)

Queen's Park Savannah	52
Simpson House	53
BP Headquarters/Queen's Park Hotel	54
Knowsley	56
National Museum and Art Gallery	57
War Memorial in War Memorial Park	58

7 Queen's Park Savannah Area (West)

All Saints Church	59
The Gingerbread House	60
The 'Magnificent Seven' Buildings	61
Queen's Royal College	61
Hayes Court	63
Milles Fleurs	64
Roomor	65
Archbishop's House	66
White Hall	67
Stollmeyer's Castle (Killarney)	68

8 Queen's Park Savannah Area (North)

President's House	70
The Botanic Gardens	71
The Hollow	73
Belmont Hill/Trinidad Hilton	74
Queen's Hall	75

9 Port of Spain West

Queen's Park Oval	76
Briar's End	77
(Former) Roxy Cinema	78
St James Barracks and Police Commissioner's House	79
Paschim Kaashi Mandir	80
Haji Gokool Meah Memorial Masjid	81
St James Medical Complex	82
Woodbrook (Mucurapo) Cemetery	83
Hasely Crawford Stadium and Jean Pierre Sports Complex	85
Fort George	87

10 Maraval

Trinidad Country Club	88
Glossary	91
Bibliography	95
Index	97

v

To Sandra

Foreword

It is a pleasure to welcome the appearance of this beautifully illustrated book on the historical buildings and sites of Port of Spain, the capital of Trinidad and Tobago, by renowned novelist and historian Michael Anthony.

Starting its life as a little collection of fishermen's huts on the coast of the Gulf of Paria; becoming the chief port and then the official capital of a growing Spanish colony towards the end of the eighteenth century (a port of Spain, indeed); transformed by the entry of French settlers, white and mixed-race, with enslaved people from the French Caribbean and directly from Africa; developing into a bustling, cosmopolitan mercantile centre under British rule in the nineteenth century – Port of Spain was, and is, the heart of political, commercial, educational and cultural life in the twin-island state which became independent in 1962. This book is about the visible legacies of these historical developments, the built heritage in Trinidad and Tobago's capital city.

No building existing in Port of Spain today is more than two hundred years old. Yet there is a wide range of architectural styles to be found in the city, if you know where to look; and many places of historical interest, if you are pointed towards them. A modern city, Port of Spain has many gems of buildings from the nineteenth and twentieth centuries which are worth more than a casual look. This book opens our eyes to the diversity and charm of this city, and will be of great interest both to the more thoughtful visitors and to the growing number of citizens and residents seriously interested in our national patrimony.

Indeed, Michael Anthony's book reminds us of how much we have lost. So much of old Port of Spain has gone for ever over the last fifty years of rapid urban development, much of which has been unplanned, and rarely informed by a historical awareness. The book highlights the fragility of our built heritage and the urgent need for the preservation of what remains. It should be a valuable tool for the newly formed National Trust of Trinidad and Tobago, and other groups concerned with the conservation of our built and natural environment. May it help us all – policy-makers, concerned citizens and residents, visitors to our country – to become more aware that our identity and integrity as a nation and a people depend, at least in part, on how we care for the visible legacies of our history and culture.

Bridget Brereton
The University of the West Indies
St Augustine Campus
Trinidad and Tobago

Trinidad and Tobago

Greater Port of Spain area

Street plan of Central Port of Spain

Queen's Park Savannah and Port of Spain West

Introduction

In their own silent way the historical landmarks of Port of Spain tell a rich and colourful story of the town from its inception until today. In fact, the story is told from the times when it was not a town at all, but a straggling little Amerindian village called Puerto de los Españoles, or 'Port of the Spaniards'.

This name might seem to have been unnecessary because it was obvious that after Cristóbal Colón claimed the island for Spain when he encountered it in 1498, it followed that everything in it was 'of the Spaniards'. So why 'Port of the Spaniards?'

The name itself throws light on the early history of the town, for it arose because the sea-dogs, the pirates and corsairs, the explorers and privateers of other nations, could not help but frequent this sheltered harbour in droves. True, they wanted to replenish their wood and water supplies, but the main reason they crowded to Puerto de los Españoles was to plot and scheme to raid the various little settlements just across the gulf on the Spanish Main, and indeed to waylay and plunder the gold and silver fleet that often left Santa Fé de Bogotá for Spain. And also, in this period when El Dorado blazed in the thoughts of all these daring men, what other spot was more convenient for a lay-over than Trinidad? So the name came from the Spanish sea-dogs who wanted the port free to do their own scheming. In their minds, the 'foreign' pirates had no right to be there since it was a 'port of the Spaniards'.

As has been said, Port of Spain's landmarks seem to recount a history without words. The story of Fort San Andrés, for instance, is bound up not only with the last of the Spanish days, but especially with the presence of French culture in Trinidad. Even at the beginning of the twenty-first century French culture and customs seem such an intrinsic part of the life of this island that it would be the easiest thing for the outsider to think mistakenly that this country once belonged to France. There is much in the cuisine that is French, and a lot of the expressions in people's speech stem from the French; many of the place-names as well as the names of rivers are French, and most intriguing of all is that French patois, as a language, is still spoken in several parts of Trinidad.

The Cedula of Population of 1783, a measure leading to the influx of French planters with their thousands of slaves immigrating to settle (and change) this country has no monument of itself to show, but it was the French planter, Philippe-Rose Roume de St Laurent, coming to Trinidad to see if he would like it, who not only fell madly in love with it, but devised the Cedula which led to the presence of the French. And it was Philippe Roume who told us of the old fort. He wrote: 'It is on the west coast that the Spaniards settle themselves, at the place where one lands, called Puerto España. Here there are several guns in a battery en barbette, a church, and about eighty houses made of roseaux, plastered with a mixture

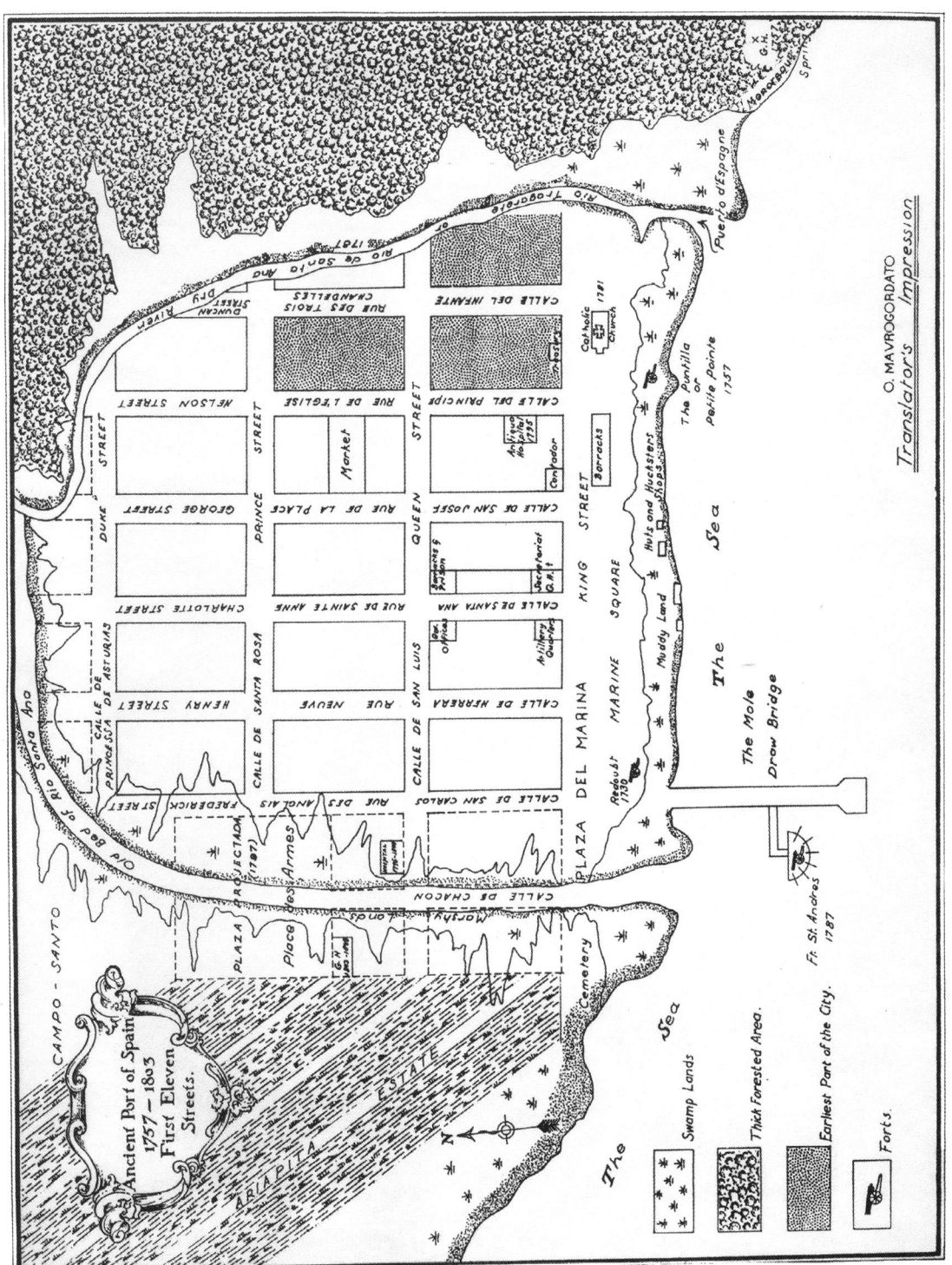

Port of Spain 1757–1803. Created by Olga J. Mavrogordato, based on descriptions in Borde's The History of Trinidad under the Spanish Government

of mud and grass then whitewashed with lime-wash and covered with thatch. The Governor lives here.' The old fort is a treasured landmark which witnessed an important change.

The next interesting landmarks tell of a crucial stage in Trinidad's political development, the end of Spanish rule and the transition between Spanish and British authority. The names of some of the streets, especially King, Queen, Prince, Duke, George, Charlotte, Duncan and Nelson show emphatically enough that the British had taken over.

The landmark that is Fort Chacón paints a picture of the very end of Spanish rule, for it was to here that the British commander-in-chief General Sir Ralph Abercromby sent a message to Chacón saying he was surrounded by land and sea and offering him an honourable surrender.

The Great Port of Spain fire of 1808 all but wiped the slate clean, and cleared the way for the rebuilding of a new town, but this period brought to light the awful problem of slavery. After the abolition of slavery in 1838 the rest of the century was marked by the consequences of the Cedula of Population,

The morning of Queen Victoria's Diamond Jubilee, 1897. The scene is the junction of King Street and Frederick Street

with unrelenting hostilities between the Anglicans, represented by the establishment, and the Roman Catholics, represented by the French element, who were very much in the majority. The construction of the Catholic Holy Trinity Church in 1816–1823 led to that of the Catholic Church of the Immaculate Conception in 1816–1832; and the founding of the Catholic institutions of St Joseph's Convent in 1836 and St Mary's College in 1863 paved the way for the establishment of the Queen's Collegiate in 1859 and Queen's Royal College in 1870. The religious 'war' raged throughout the period when the colleges were being erected.

The principal event of the final years of the century was one which was literally to take Port of Spain from the darkness into light. This was the establishment of the electric works in 1895 in a little pasture (Shine's Pasture) by Edgar Tripp, who successfully brought electricity to Port of Spain. The fact that those electric works are on the same spot today is a fascinating part of the story.

The conflict between Anglicans and Catholics led to the erection of one landmark, the new Red House (government offices) in 1907; the earlier building was destroyed by fire in 1903 during the religious 'war', and lay as rubble on the ground for some time. Sir Henry MacLeod had laid the foundation stone of this building in 1844. (Sir Henry MacLeod was the governor who introduced the most inflammatory period of the 'war' by first abolishing the Illustrious Cabildo in 1840.) After the British had conquered Trinidad in 1797, the Cabildo, or Spanish Town Council, was retained by a special agreement between General Sir Ralph Abercromby and the defeated Spanish governor Don José María Chacón. MacLeod had then introduced English laws and trial by jury, and, perhaps the greatest blow of all, he brought in the Ecclesiastical Ordinance (1844), which made the Anglican Church the State Church at the expense of the Catholic Church).

In terms of the development of the country, the Trinidad Government Railway, which was introduced in 1876, established an imposing landmark in Port of Spain in 1924 when Railway Headquarters on Lower Frederick Street was built. Oddly enough, this period marked the beginning of the end for the Trinidad Government Railway. It could not withstand motor competition, which was mainly from taxis and buses, and it lost so much money that by 1930 it had become a liability to the government.

But Trinidad was progressing all the time, on every front, despite failures, and the story had to be told. On the political front, it marched to independence in 1962, and a relevant physical landmark is the statue of one of the stoutest fighters for independence, Captain Arthur Andrew Cipriani. It was progressing on the industrial front and on the commercial front, too, and perhaps the final landmark that should be mentioned is one of the newest represented in this book: the twin towers of the Eric Williams Financial Complex.

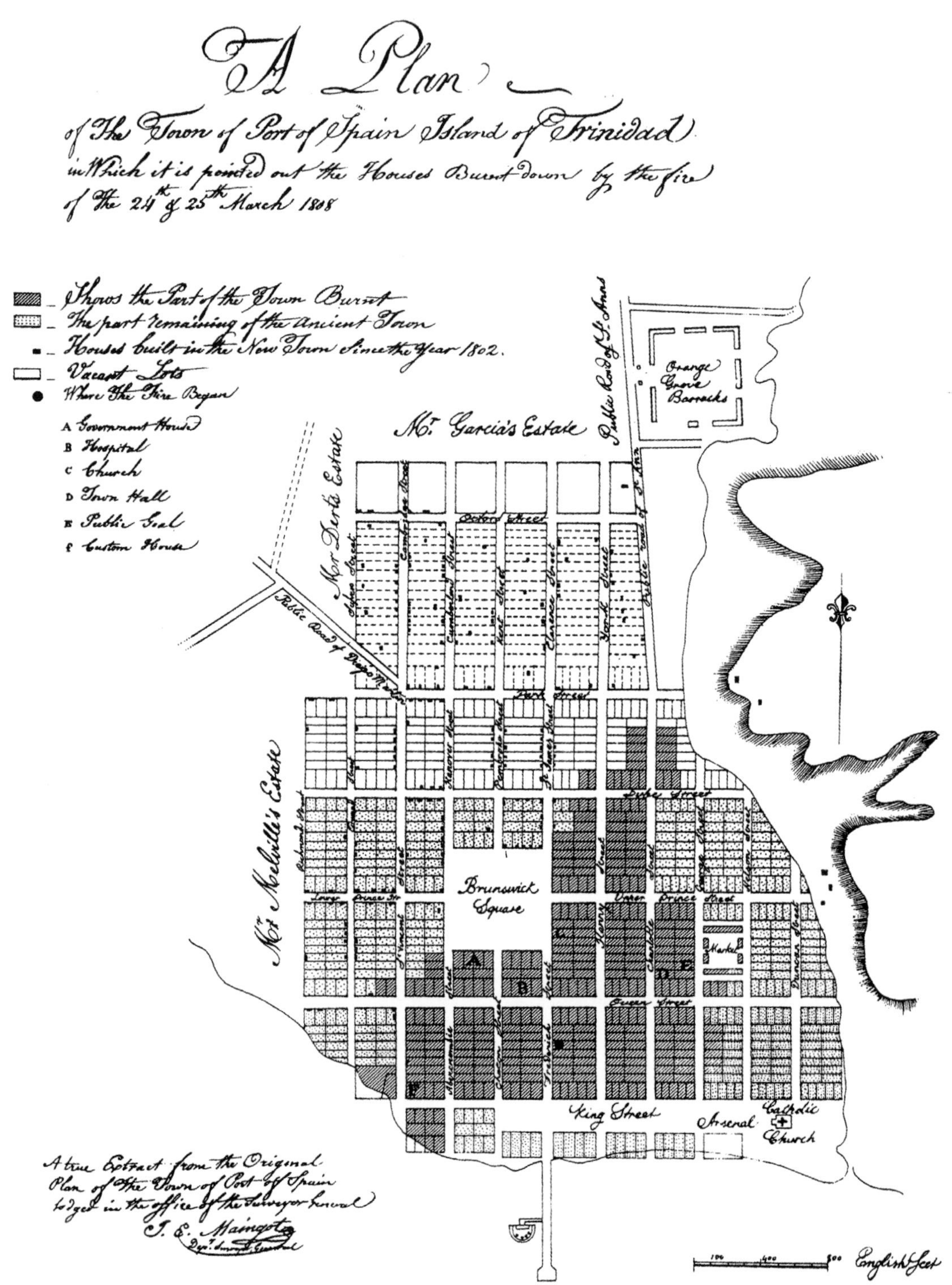

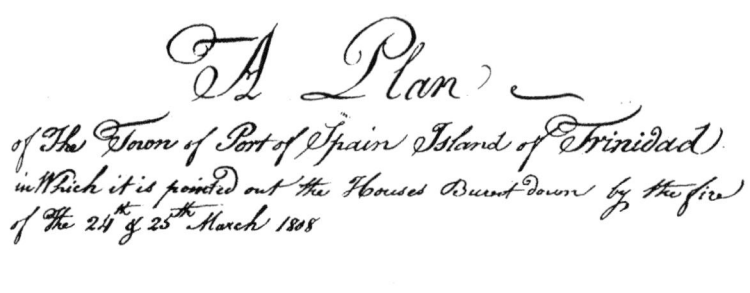

Port of Spain 1808, showing the expansion of the town in the first decade of the nineteenth century and the devastation caused by the Great Fire of 1808

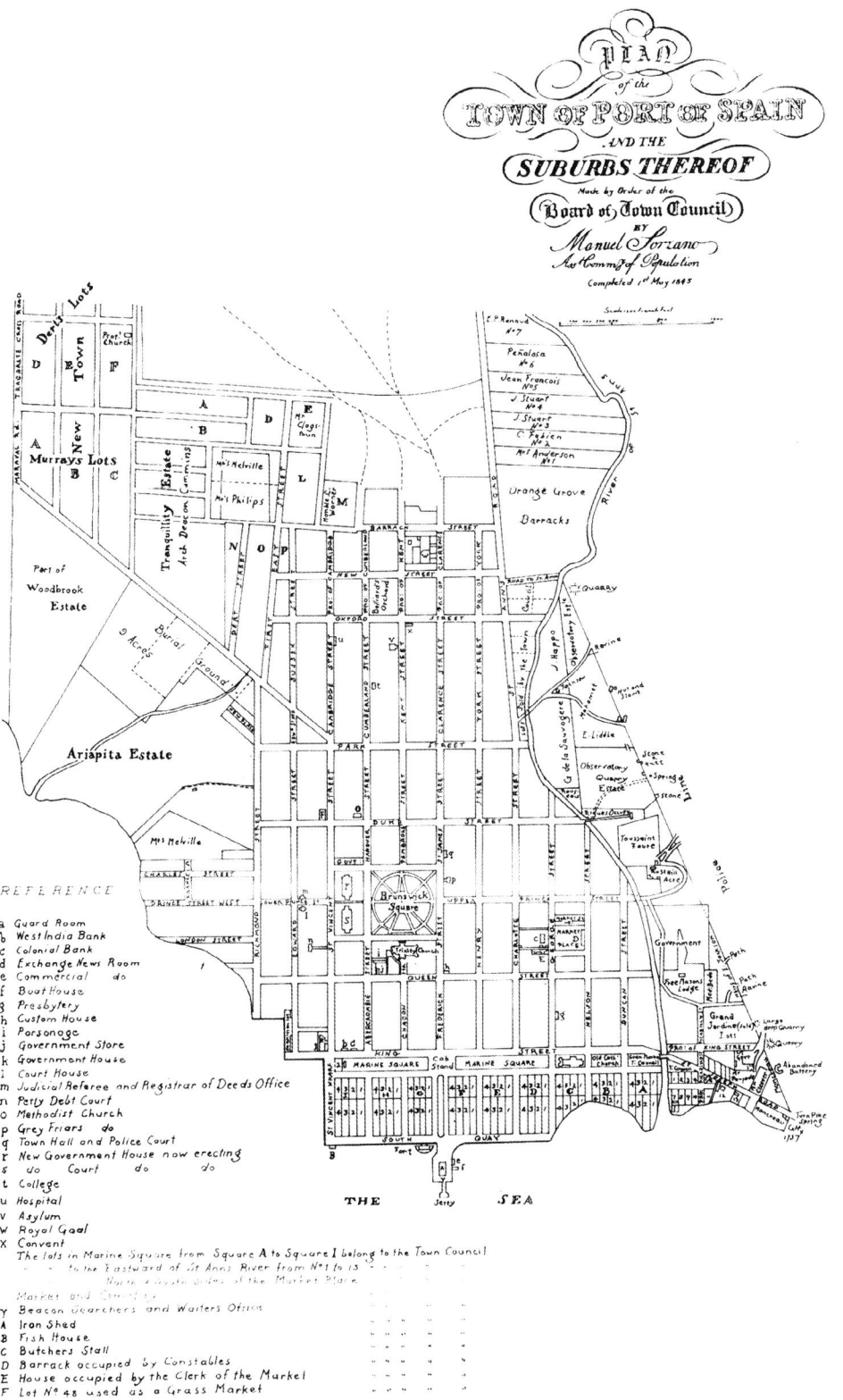

Port of Spain 1845, showing the expansion of the town westwards and southwards, with Fort San Andrés no longer surrounded by water

There are more than sixty of Port of Spain's treasured landmarks in this book, each telling a story. A look at the historic landmarks of Port of Spain will introduce the reader to a rewarding pictorial history of the city.

Note: Architectural terms given in italic are explained in the Glossary.

1 Central Port of Spain (Independence Square, South Quay, and the Waterfront)

Independence Square and Brian Lara Promenade

Independence Square lies at the heart of downtown Port of Spain and stretches for almost three-quarters of a mile (1 kilometre) from the St Ann's (or Dry) River in the east to Wrightson Road in the west. The Brian Lara Promenade, named in honour of the famous cricketer, runs almost the full length of the square, from Richmond Street to George Street. Designed by local architect Colin Laird, the promenade was laid out between 1993 and 1995. The Roman Catholic Cathedral of the Immaculate Conception, completed in 1832 (the oldest existing building on the square), anchors the eastern end of

Brian Lara Promenade with the Eric Williams Financial Complex in the background

The Nicholas Tower, Independence Square

the promenade, while the Eric Williams Financial Complex, opened in 1986, dominates the western end. A statue of Arthur Cipriani, the renowned Labour leader, sits in the middle of the square, at the southern end of Frederick Street. Notable on the north side of the square, between Edward and St Vincent Streets, is the Treasury, built in 1838. Once nearby was the distinctive Ice House, but it was torn down in 1977. Buildings of interest that once graced the square on the south were the Colonial Bank (1837) and the Union Club. The latter was designed by the Scottish architect George Brown. Brown was responsible for creating most of the major buildings erected in Port of Spain after a devastating downtown fire in 1895. The Union Club building was demolished in 1999 to make way for the 21-floor Nicholas Tower.

The Union Club building once stood at the south-east corner of Abercromby Street and today's Independence Square South

The area at the north-eastern end of the square, near the cathedral, is of particular historical importance because it was the nucleus of today's city. It became the administrative centre of the colonial government when Port of Spain was made the capital of Spanish Trinidad in 1784 (inland San José, now St Joseph, had served that function until then for nearly two hundred years, since 1592). Public buildings such as the treasury, the court house, the military barracks, the prison, and the residence of the governor himself were arrayed along the then-few streets of the town such as Calle de la Marina (today's Independence Square north); Calle Santa Ana (today's Charlotte Street); Calle del Príncipe (now Nelson);

The Ice House at Abercromby Street and today's Independence Square North

The Colonial Bank after it was moved to Marine Square, today's Independence Square South.

and Calle del Infante (today's Duncan). In the late eighteenth century, these streets extended only three blocks north of Calle de la Marina, to Calle Princesa de Asturias (today's Duke Street). A small church was located a block east of the present cathedral. At the time, the sea came right up to the area called Plaza de la Marina (today's Independence Square), which the British renamed Marine Square after they took over Trinidad in 1797. (Beginning in 1803, and for the next two decades, reclamation southward occurred, reaching as far as South Quay by the 1830s.) The British also changed the name of Calle de la Marina to King Street, a name it retained until 1961, when it became Independence Square North. Marine Square was renamed Independence Square when Trinidad and Tobago achieved independence in 1962.

Marine Square West, 1900

Fort San Andrés/City Museum of Port of Spain

Now the City Museum of Port of Spain, this recently restored building was originally built in the early nineteenth century as a customs house, with additions made in the course of the following fifty years or so to accommodate reading and meeting rooms for merchants in the area.

As early as 1730, there was reference to a fortification at or near this site: a simple *reducto*, or redoubt, was described by the Spanish governor of the time as 'made of fascines [bundles of sticks] and earth covered by palm leaves'. If it was at this site, the redoubt would then have been offshore; if not, it was probably on the shore itself, close to where the statue of Arthur Cipriani stands today, in Independence Square. In any event, by the 1770s there existed on this site a more substantial fortification, with a 4½-metre (15-foot) high crescent-shaped wall. This fort was in the sea but joined by a drawbridge to the western side of a 212-metre (700-foot) long, 9-metre (30-foot) wide pier. (This pier ran the length of today's Broadway, then unreclaimed from the sea.) The fortification was called Fort San Andrés, a response by the Spanish authorities to aggressive British naval activity in the Caribbean. Visiting Trinidad in 1777, Philippe-Rose Roume de St Laurent, a French Grenadian, noted that the fort had 'several guns in a *batterie en barbette*', a reference to cannon arrayed to shoot over a parapet, an arrangement which can still be seen today on the southern side of the building (the original high wall is now much reduced as a result of landfill and reclamations). A plan of the time shows a total of 11 cannons facing the sea, but this defence proved to be woefully inadequate when the British invaded Trinidad in 1797, and the fort fell into ruin in the early part of the nineteenth century. By 1845, land reclamation had advanced the waterfront to meet the site of the fort, and further reclamation in the decades following 1850 resulted in its being completely cut off from the sea, as it is today.

In addition to the business, reading and meeting rooms, the existing building has over the past century and a half housed the harbourmaster's office, the Trinidad and Tobago Chamber of Commerce, and the Traffic Branch of the Police Service. The first meridian in the Americas, it should be noted, was established on this site in August 1792 (see Fort Chacón, page 19).

Fort San Andrés today

Cathedral of the Immaculate Conception

Records show that a Catholic church existed as early as 1781 in Tamarind Square, just behind the location of today's cathedral. The original church was a simple structure built of mud and grass with a thatched roof of palm leaves. By the turn of the century, this had been replaced by a larger wooden structure, described by the nineteenth-century Trinidadian historian Pierre Gustave Borde as 'plain, rectangular in shape, 80 feet by 48 including the sacristy … [with] a capacity of 450-500 people … [and] there were "galleries"'. The church faced Plaza de la Marina, the heart of the town. Close by – on the northern side of the plaza and just around the corner on streets now called Nelson, George, and Charlotte – were structures such as the treasury, prison, and hospital, the main public buildings of Puerto de España, which became the official capital of Spanish Trinidad in 1784. Immediately to the south of the church was the shoreline, which was not extended by reclamation to its present position until the second and subsequent decades of the nineteenth century.

Much of this land reclamation occurred during the governorship of Sir Ralph Woodford (1813–1828), who was also

Lithograph by Richard Bridgens of the Cathedral in 1832

responsible for the building of the church that exists today. Woodford laid its foundation stone on 24 March 1816, just two months before he did the same for the town's main Anglican church, Holy Trinity. The Catholic church was meant to serve the predominantly Catholic population of Port of Spain, but they were a long time in the waiting; the church was not completed until 1832

An example of the nineteenth-century *Gothic Revival* – or 'second-order Gothic', in the words of Archbishop Smith – the cathedral is built mainly of brick imported from England and local blue limestone from Laventille, the hill just a kilometre (half a mile) east of the building. Its distinctive two towers were originally all stone, but, after they were damaged in an earthquake in 1825, their top parts were rebuilt in wood. These contain 12 bells. The church is shaped like a Latin cross, with a nave measuring some 24 metres (80 feet) by 24 metres. Behind and above the high altar is a stained-glass window depicting Our Lady of Lourdes. The high altar itself, made of marble, was installed in 1966. It replaced one of Florentine marble, which, along with carved communion rails of the same material, now sits in the Chapel of Our Lady on the northern side of the cathedral. In this chapel there is also a plaque in memory of Sir Ralph Woodford, with the inscription:

'The inhabitants have caused this monument to be erected as a lasting memorial to his many public and private virtues.'

Beneath the Chapel of St Joseph on the southern side of the cathedral there is a crypt where prominent clerics of the local Catholic church are buried, including the first local archbishop, Anthony Pantin.

The cathedral can seat around 1500 people.

The Cathedral today

The Port of Spain Lighthouse

When it was constructed in 1842 at a cost of $4,600, the 18.2 metre (60-foot) high Port of Spain lighthouse, located at the bottom of today's Broadway, was the tallest structure in the town. It was built to deal with the increasing number of vessels plying the Port of Spain harbour. This sea traffic was attracted by growth in commercial establishments south of Marine (now Independence) Square, the consequence of land reclamations in the 1820s and 1830s.

No longer functional, the lighthouse seems to have been problematic from its earliest days. On 17 July 1846, four years after it was built, the editor of the *Port of Spain Gazette* wrote sourly: 'If it were useful but inexpensive, or useless but costing a mere trifle, the thing might be tolerated, but to see a considerable sum of money lavished annually on such a mockery of the valuable invention it is meant to represent is really too bad, and argues little for the spirit of the judgement of our municipality.'

The structure started leaning in the early 1960s as a result of excavations to install a new sewage system in the city.

Columbus Square

Located just east of the Cathedral of the Immaculate Conception, this square and its statue honour Christopher Columbus, who encountered Trinidad in 1498, on his third voyage. The square was laid out in 1880–1 and the statue itself, erected when the square was opened, was a gift of Hippolyte Borde, a wealthy local cacao planter and merchant.

South Quay and the Waterfront

South Quay today is a road which runs east–west a block north of the Port of Spain waterfront, from St Vincent Street to the St Ann's (Dry) River. The road was built on land reclamations that were started in 1803 and which were, in a first phase, to extend the waterfront southwards from Marine (now Independence) Square. The 1845 map on page xvii shows South Quay directly bordering the sea and extending from St Vincent Street to George Street, two blocks short of the river. In the 1850s, further reclamations expanded the waterfront south and westwards. These filled in the area now known as City Gate and housing the old Railway Headquarters.

Saint Vincent Street Wharf looking north, c. 1900

Old Custom House and Harbourmaster's Office, which stood on the waterfront from 1880 to 1980

Railway Headquarters Building/ City Gate

Built in 1924, the Railway Headquarters Building stands at the south-eastern corner of Broadway and South Quay. The now-defunct Trinidad Government Railway had actually been inaugurated nearly fifty years earlier, on 30 August 1876, with a service between Port of Spain and St Joseph, which was extended farther east to Arima in the same year. The building that served as the railway station for most of these earlier years is shown below in a photograph taken around 1916.

The Railway Headquarters Building, 1916

The railway was scrapped bit by bit from 1954 to 1968 and the existing building now serves as the headquarters of the Public Transport Service Corporation and as the hub of City Gate, the main gateway for public transport to and from Port of Spain. An example of British Imperial public architecture, the building is notable for neo-classical details such as the use of *pediments* supported by pilasters of the Tuscan *order*.

City Gate

The Cipriani Statue

This statue of Captain Arthur Andrew Cipriani was unveiled on 17 April 1959 by the then Chief Minister, Dr Eric Williams, as a tribute to the great Labour leader. It is a popular landmark, standing as it does at Port of Spain's busiest intersection, Independence Square North with Frederick Street. In the late nineteenth century this spot was the site of a fountain which depicted a young boy with his hand around the neck of a swan. However, in 1900, the fountain was removed to facilitate the laying-down of rails for the city's growing electrical tram system.

Cipriani was born in 1875 in Port of Spain, the descendant of Corsican immigrants who had come to Trinidad at the end of the eighteenth century. He was a captain of the West India Regiment and served in the Middle East during World War I. He made his greatest impact after returning from the war in 1919, when he defended the rights of veterans and others who were exploited or unemployed as a result of the post-war recession. Cipriani soon became known as 'the champion of the barefoot man', advancing the cause of the country's working classes through his strong union leadership and through politics: he was president of the Trinidad Workingman's Association, which became the Trinidad Labour Party in 1934; a member of the Port of Spain City Council and the Legislative Council over a period of 24 years; and mayor of Port of Spain for all but two years between 1929 and 1940. Cipriani died on 18 April 1945.

The statue of Cipriani at the intersection of Frederick Street and Independence Square

The Treasury Building

This building, which now houses departments of Trinidad and Tobago's Ministry of Finance, was for many years the Treasury and the General Post Office. Located on Independence Square north, between Edward and St Vincent Streets, the foundation stone of this structure, the major public building erected in Port of Spain in the 1930s, was laid in 1936 and its construction completed in 1938. It replaced an earlier building containing the Treasury and the government rum bond that burned down in the early hours of 25 June 1932, resulting in the destruction of some 15,000 casks of rum. A contemporary report of the fire in the *Trinidad Guardian* described 'a huge blazing river of rum' flowing down to the waterfront, 'setting the sea literally on fire'. This newer building, notable for the symmetrically arranged flat arches in its front elevation, was designed by Hubert Brinsley, a British

The Modern Treasury

architect who also designed the Globe cinema. The original Treasury and Rum Bond building constructed by Sir Lewis Grant in 1831 also gave some of its space to Sir Lewis to be used as government offices. It was from here that Governor Sir George Fitzgerald Hill, who succeeded Grant, declared the emancipation of the slaves in 1834 and the abolition of slavery in 1838. It was also from here that Governor Sir Henry MacLeod, Hill's successor, presided over the laying of the foundation stone of new government offices not far away; these offices became the 'Red House' by the end of the nineteenth century. Lord Harris, who succeeded MacLeod in 1846, also came to reside in this building. After opening the new government offices in 1848, he left in 1852, came back, and finally left in 1854. It is believed that Harris's successor, Charles Elliot, and the following Governor, William Keate, also lived here, but the residency of governors in the Treasury and Rum Bond definitely closed with the advent of Sir Arthur Gordon.

It must be said that the presence of the Treasury and Rum Bond building on this spot as late as 1932 shows that until further land reclamations were made in the early twentieth century, this block was on the edge of the waterfront.

The Eric Williams Financial Complex

The Eric Williams Financial Complex, located at the south-western end of Independence Square, consists of two 22-storey buildings: the Central Bank Tower, which contains the offices of the Central Bank of Trinidad and Tobago; and the Eric Williams Finance Building, which houses the Ministry of Finance, the Department of the Auditor General, and the Ministry of Planning and Development. The latter building and the complex itself are named after Dr Eric Williams, the distinguished Caribbean historian and politician who led the country to independence from the United Kingdom in 1962. Construction of the complex started in 1979 and was completed in 1986 at a cost of just over TT$200 million. It has two areas for public performances: an open-air courtyard and an auditorium in the Central Bank Tower.

The Eric Williams Financial Complex

Colonial Life Building

Trinidad and Tobago's first 'skyscraper', the 31-metre (103-foot) high Colonial Life building on lower St Vincent Street, was opened in 1954 after two years of construction. Its first four floors rise straight up from street level one above the other, while the remaining two floors form ziggurat-type 'steps' of diminishing dimensions that produce the effect of a central tower. The slightly recessed main entrance to the building stands at the bottom of this 'tower', directly in the middle of the front elevation. The entrance rises two floors and the crest of the Colonial Life Insurance Company (CLICO) appears prominently above the main doors. The entrance is framed in black marble, a material that also clads the front exterior of the entire first floor. The intent is to present an imposing public face, befitting the headquarters of the country's first local insurance company, established by Cyril Duprey in 1936. CLICO now has extensive investments throughout the Caribbean in insurance, real estate, banking, and other business sectors.

2 Central Port of Spain (East)

United Brothers Masonic Lodge

A Masonic lodge has stood on this site since 1804. First known as the home of *Les Frères Unis* freemasons, the original building survived Port of Spain's Great Fire of 1808, but was seriously damaged by another fire in 1837. The reconstructed building that we see today retains the simple but dignified façade of the original: a main porch fronted by three wide depressed arches surmounted by a *pediment* in the style of a Classical temple.

Lithograph of the Lodge by Richard Bridgens, 1831

United Brothers Masonic Lodge

Fort Chacón

Now a police telecommunications site, Fort Chacón, on the Laventille Road overlooking Port of Spain, is named after the last Spanish governor of Trinidad, Don José María Chacón. He is said to have retreated here on 17 February 1797 as the British advanced on Port of Spain, but he surrendered quickly in the face of the enemy's overwhelming military might. The structure on the site today is probably the remains of an observatory that Chacón had built in 1792 for Don Cosme Damian de Churruca, a naval officer and astronomer who came to Trinidad in June that year. Don Cosme led an expedition intending to map and fix meridians in Trinidad and other places in Spanish America.

Fort Picton

Fort Picton, located on the Laventille Hill, was built in 1803 by Sir Thomas Picton, the first British governor of Trinidad. The fort was popularly referred to as Picton's Folly, as it was never actually used to defend Port of Spain. The fort is 9 metres (30 feet) high and its circular shape makes it an example of a *Martello tower*, a common form of coastal defence in Britain during the Napoleonic Wars (1803–15).

L'Hospice of St Vincent de Paul

L'Hospice of St Vincent de Paul has been at this site on Observatory Street in east Port of Spain since 1858, when the original buildings, no longer existing, were constructed under the direction of the Italian-born Roman Catholic Archbishop of Port of Spain, Vincent Spaccapietra. This occurred in the wake of a devastating cholera epidemic in 1854. Now the oldest home for the aged in Trinidad, the institution originally housed people left ill and homeless by the epidemic, which killed just over 10 per cent of Port of Spain's population (20,000 at the time). Over the years, L'Hospice has been run by two Catholic organisations, the St Vincent de Paul Society (whose Trinidad branch Archbishop Spaccapietra founded) and, since 1934, the Carmelite nuns. A Latin inscription across the front gate of the building honours Archbishop Spaccapietra and his work.

The Drinking Trough

This drinking trough for donkeys, mules, cattle, and horses lies on the Eastern Main Road, in east Port of Spain. Inscribed on it is an *H* and the year *1853*, which clearly dates it to the time of Governor Lord Harris. It is the only remaining such trough in Port of Spain, and was also the last one at which animals with their riders, herdsmen and agricultural produce would stop before entering the city from the east. The sign on the wall behind the trough reads: 'This drinking trough was erected in the administration of Lord Harris in 1853 for the purpose of enabling horses, mules and other animals to quench their thirst as they came to the end of their journey to Port of Spain.'

3 Central Port of Spain (Woodford Square Area)

Woodford Square

Surrounded by the country's most important public buildings such as the Red House, the Hall of Justice, and the National Library, Woodford Square is named after Sir Ralph Woodford, who was the British governor of Trinidad from 1813 to 1828. His name was not, however, given to this much-used public space until 1917, when it was changed from Brunswick Square. Originally laid out during Woodford's governorship, the square was named Brunswick after a German regiment from Brunswick which came to Trinidad with the British invading forces.

The area in which the square is located was originally part of the course of the St Ann's River, which, until 1787, wound its way from the hills north of Port of Spain down to the Gulf of Paria. (Today's Chacon Street, directly south of the square, was also part of the course.) In 1787, Don José María Chacón, the last Spanish governor of Trinidad, had the river diverted in its lower reaches to the eastern part of the town, where it remains today and is commonly

The fountain in Woodford Square. This picture, taken in the square at the turn of the nineteenth century, shows the very ornate fountain. It was presented to Port of Spain by Gregor Turnbull of the Trinidad Trading Company Limited.

called the Dry River. It came to be used as a military parade ground. Between its reclamation and its being officially named Brunswick Square, the area was informally called Place des Armes by the largely French-speaking population of early British Port of Spain.

The fountain in the centre of the square was donated in 1866 by Gregor Turnbull, a Glasgow-born local merchant. The tall railings around the square were installed in 1892, while the bandstand was built and opened in 1917, the same year that the square got its present name. The bandstand has served as a stage for performances by the African-American singers Paul Robeson (in 1948) and Marion Anderson (in 1960), and by Trinidad and Tobago's own world-renowned pianist Winifred Atwell in 1969. Most famously, the square became known as the 'University of Woodford Square' in the 1956–62 period, when it was used by Dr Eric Williams and his People's National Movement (PNM) as a forum for mass public rallies leading up to independence from the United Kingdom in 1962.

The square continues to be a popular place, used as it is for relaxation and entertainment, as a pedestrian link between the many important public buildings and businesses in the area, and for informal political debates and large demonstrations. During the most clamorous of these, the Black Power protests of 1970, the square picked up yet another unofficial name, the 'People's Parliament'.

The Red House

In 1844, governor Sir Henry MacLeod laid the foundation stone for new government offices, the existing ones being in the Treasury and Rum Bond. The greater part of these new brick structures was completed in 1848 and opened by the governor of the time, Lord Harris. They were designed by Richard Bridgens, Superintendent of Public Works, and consisted of two distinct buildings, linked by a triple archway over Lower Prince Street (now Sackville Street). The building to the south was for the law courts and registry, and the building to the north eventually housed the chamber of the Legislative Council.

In the course of the second half of the nineteenth century there were several modifications to the building, and in 1897 the two buildings, which were then one, were painted in 'patriotic' red to mark the Diamond Jubilee of Queen Victoria. From this period, it became known as the Red House.

The Red House was seriously gutted by fire during the Water Riots of 1903. It was rebuilt in its existing form at a cost of almost £48,000, designed and constructed under the supervision of the Chief Draughtsman of Public Works, Daniel Mienerts Hahn. Hahn also designed Queen's Royal College. The Red House was reopened in 1907, and since then has housed the legislative bodies of Trinidad and Tobago, as well as other key branches and offices of government. Its front courtyard (facing St Vincent Street), was the scene of the flag-raising ceremony to mark Independence Day, 31 August 1962.

A particularly dramatic event in the history of the Red House took place on 27 July 1990, when members of a Black Muslim group, the Jamaat al Muslimeen, burst into the chamber of the House of Representatives and held the prime minister and other members of the house hostage there for six days in an attempted coup d'état. A truce was eventually reached, but the parliamentary chamber and other parts of the building suffered damage as a result of the exchange of gunfire with police and militia trying to retake the building.

The Red House as it exists today has been loosely described as 'French Renaissance' in style and is distinguished on the outside by its high central dome, which covers a rotunda located in what used to be the roadway between the two original buildings. The almost 34-metre (110-foot) high dome was originally crowned

The Red House today

by the figure of a sea serpent, but this was replaced in 1992 with a copper dove bearing an olive branch. (This was designed by the late Ken Morris, a well-known metalworker and Carnival bandleader.) Neo-classical *pediments* supported by columns of the Corinthian and Composite *orders* are also notable exterior features of the building (for example, its southern end, on the east elevation). The chamber of the House of Representatives has a striking Wedgwood-blue ceiling with *gesso* work, and a Speaker's dais and *entablature* designed by Daniel Mienerts Hahn and made of purpleheart wood. The chamber also contains busts honouring Arthur Cipriani, the renowned Labour leader, and Sir Louis de Verteuil. Sir Louis was a nineteenth-century leader of the local French Creole community and first mayor, in 1853, of the Borough of Port of Spain.

Illustration by Cabazon, 1849, of the early government buildings

Trinity Cathedral

Today's Anglican Cathedral, which dominates the block south of Woodford Square, has two precursors: the first was a small wooden church at the corner of Frederick and Prince Streets. It burned to the ground in the fire of 1808 that destroyed most of Port of Spain. In its place, construction of a second church began in Brunswick Square (as Woodford Square was then called), but, after public protests, this was never completed. The foundation stone of the current church was laid on 30 May 1816, and the building was completed in 1818. However, it was not consecrated until Trinity Sunday, 25 May 1823, in the presence of the British governor of Trinidad at the time, Sir Ralph Woodford. His Colonial Secretary, Philip Reinagle, an architect, was responsible for its design (as he was also for that of the city's Roman Catholic Cathedral). Trinity Cathedral, formerly part of the Diocese of Barbados, became an independent church in 1872.

The cathedral is a mix of late *Georgian*, nineteenth-century *Gothic Revival* and Victorian styles, and is built of imported bricks and local blue limestone quarried in Laventille, the

Trinity Cathedral today

hill overlooking east Port of Spain. The Georgian characteristics of the church are evident in the neo-classical simplicity of the nave. Gothic Revival features are particularly striking in its carved *hammer-beam* mahogany ceiling, said to be inspired by that of Westminster Hall in London, and in the pointed arch windows. The chancel – built in 1897 as a memorial to Bishop Richard Rawle, the first Anglican Bishop of Trinidad – reflects the Victorian era, particularly in its stained glass. The main altar, built in 1927, is made of local mahogany, backed by alabaster, and stands on a base of Portland stone. Wall tablets commemorate some of the members of Trinidad's nineteenth-century British elite, including one to Lady Sarah Harris, daughter of a former archdeacon of the church, and wife of Lord Harris, the island's governor from 1846 to 1854.

The most notable monument in the cathedral is one to Sir Ralph Woodford, in the form of a life-size, semi-recumbent marble figure by renowned early nineteenth-century British sculptor Sir Francis Legatt Chantrey, whose work also appears in St Paul's Cathedral and Westminster Abbey. The most outstanding features on the exterior of the building are its tower and octagonal steeple, both restored after being badly damaged in an earthquake in 1825. They contain one of the church's original bells, dated 1819.

The cathedral can seat about 1200 people.

Chantrey monument of Woodford

Hall of Justice

The Hall of Justice, located on Knox Street, just north of Woodford Square, was designed by the local firm of Anthony C. Lewis Associates and opened in 1985. It contains the Court of Appeal, the Civil and Criminal Divisions of the High Court, the Supreme Court Law Library, and the Tax Appeal Board. All courts are on the first floor, ranged around the Main Court Hall. The library is on the third floor. On the outside, this ultra-modern building is clad in pre-cast concrete panels with exposed stone aggregate. It takes up an entire city block, at the south-western end of which stood the arcaded Lucien Building, a local landmark, which was torn down in the late 1970s to make way for the new building.

The Hall of Justice

The Lucien Building

City Hall

This is the seat of municipal government for the City of Port of Spain. The foundation stone for the building was laid in 1958 by Princess Margaret of the United Kingdom, and it was opened on 27 October 1961. The city has been administered from this site since 1898. In that year, the offices of the Borough of Port of Spain settled into an outstanding example of early nineteenth-century Spanish-style colonial architecture, which, unfortunately, burned down in 1948. Between 1948 and 1961, the city's administration was temporarily housed in the Prince's Building, south of the Queen's Park Savannah (now also destroyed by fire).

City Hall

Old Library Building

Completed in early 1902 – although the roof-top pediment above the main entrance bears the date 1901 – this library building was opened on Friday 21 March 1902. Ornate, with its distinctive second floor gallery arches, the library, which in recent times became known as the Heritage Library, served until 2003 as the city's main public library. The earliest public library in Trinidad was set up in 1851, founded by governor Lord Harris, and over the next fifty years it was housed in different places around the city, the last on Chacon Street before the move was made to this building. A bust in this building honours William George Knox, the first Trinidad-born Chief Justice of the island and a supporter of the library in its earlier days. Knox Street, on which the building is located, is named for him.

National Library

The L-shaped National Library building was opened in 2003 at a cost of TT$100 million. It serves as the headquarters of the country's National Library and Information System Authority (NALIS), which administers all public libraries in Trinidad and Tobago; and it houses the Heritage Library, as well as collections for children, young adults, and adults. Altogether it has about one million books. The seven-storey building, which has almost 2200 square metres (24,000 square feet) of floor space, was designed by local architect Colin Laird and reflects the pitched roofs and siding of indigenous architecture in its use of galvanised, or corrugated iron, in external panels and awning. The library complex boasts a circular, galleried atrium and an outdoor amphitheatre shaded by suspended sails. The amphitheatre stands next to the main entrance and helps integrate the main building with the restored Old Fire Brigade Building of 1895.

Old Fire Brigade Building

The late Victorian Old Fire Brigade Building, with its distinctive tower, was built at a cost of £4,000 in 1895–6, in the aftermath of the 1895 fire that destroyed much of downtown Port of Spain. It served for many years as the main fire station of the city, and became the headquarters of the Trinidad and Tobago Fire Service when that entity was established in 1951. (Before that, the local fire service had been run by the police.) In the late 1950s the Fire Service moved to more modern quarters on Wrightson Road and the old building fell into disrepair. It was then renovated by the Trinidad Theatre Workshop, which used it as base for a decade, from 1989 to 1999. Since then, the building has been extensively restored and it now forms part of the National Library complex, which opened in 2003.

Greyfriars Church

Alexander Kennedy, a Scot, brought Presbyterianism to Trinidad in 1836. He first held services in the Wesleyan Chapel, now the Hanover Methodist Church, at the corner of Abercromby (then called Hanover) and Duke Streets. In that same year, Kennedy relocated his church to the east side of Cambridge Street (now St Vincent Street), occupying what had been a theatre. He later moved to Frederick Street, where he built Greyfriars Church, the foundation stone having been laid on 10 April 1837. The big opening day for the church was 21 January 1838. It must have been a happy coincidence that Kennedy, who was an outspoken opponent of slavery, and president of the Trinidad Anti-Slavery Society, should open his church in the same year slavery was abolished, 1838. The building, much smaller, was enlarged to its present size in 1877, and further renovations took place in 1950. Greyfriars was named after the mother chuch, which was in Glasgow, Scotland.

Old Police Headquarters

The foundation stone for this structure was laid in 1870 and the building completed in 1876. It originally served as headquarters for both the police and the volunteer fire brigade, and contained the residence of the head of the local police force and quarters for non-commissioned officers. Situated on the site of older wooden barracks that had housed the First West India Regiment, the building cost £90,000 to complete. The main material used was limestone from the Piccadilly Quarry in east Port of Spain and the building's principal features are its square clock tower and galleries of Gothic pointed arches. The structure was seriously damaged by fire on two occasions, the first in 1881. The second fire was particularly dramatic as it was a result of firebombing on 27 July 1990 during the attempted coup d'état by the Jamaat-Al-Muslimeen. The building was completely gutted during this fire, but it has now been restored and houses the Museum of the Trinidad and Tobago Police Service.

Cabildo Building

The Cabildo was the council that administered Trinidad during Spanish rule. It was originally based in San José de Oruña (now St Joseph), 10 kilometres (6 miles) east of Port of Spain. The Cabildo started to meet in what was then Puerto España in 1784. There had been a long history of tension between the metropolitan governor and the locals, or *criollos*, of Spanish descent and when the coastal town was officially made the new capital in 1784, the Cabildo moved there permanently.

It is not known exactly where the Cabildo was first housed in the new capital, but it might have been in the north-east area of the Plaza de la Marina (today's Independence Square). In this vicinity, the whole town was made up of only about six small streets. It is known that by the time of the fire of 1808, the Cabildo was located on the east side of Charlotte Street, just north of Queen Street. With this building destroyed, the Cabildo was relocated, probably for short periods, in one or two rented premises before settling by 1837 in the building pictured here, on Sackville Street (then called Lower Prince Street). A few years later, the Cabildo moved again: an 1845 map locates it on St James Street (the name until 1902, which was the date St James Street, an extension, took the name of the original street, Frederick Street). But some of the Cabildo's functions remained behind: the same 1845 map

The outside of the Cabildo

identifies the pictured building as housing the offices of the 'Judicial Referee and Registrar of Deeds'. In the course of the rest of the nineteenth century and into the twentieth century the building was used for various municipal functions and for lawyers' offices but it fell into disrepair and was eventually abandoned. Fortunately, it was restored in 2002 and it now forms part of the Cabildo Chambers complex that houses the offices of the Attorney General and Minister of Legal Affairs of Trinidad and Tobago.

Possibly built originally as a private home, this modest one-storey building, located one block west of the Red House, has features of Spanish colonial architecture – notably a central courtyard, with a fountain that is surrounded by an arcade. Since this area of the town was not developed under the Spanish, however, the structure was probably not built until the early days of British rule, in the first decade of the nineteenth century. It is very probably the oldest building in Port of Spain today.

The restored fountain in the Cabildo courtyard

4 Central Port of Spain ('Uptown')

Globe Cinema

This quaint-looking cinema (and theatre) called the Globe, stands at the busy junction of Park Street, St Vincent Street, and Tragarete Road – a junction one might refer to as being in 'the heart of Town'. It was opened on Sunday 19 March 1933, as the Metro Cinema, apparently having been a joint effort by Metro-Goldwyn-Mayer, the American film company, and a Trinidad businessman, Gokool Meah. The architect was Hubert Brinsley, an Englishman who soon afterwards (1936) was to work on the design of the Treasury Building. The Globe was the fifth cinema in Port of Spain, and the partnership between Gokool Meah and MGM seemed set to flourish when disagreement stepped in. Metro had welcomed the partnership, seeing in the Metro Cinema an exclusive channel for its films, and although Gokool might have agreed to this initially, concerns about successful films not reaching the Metro because they were not MGM's caused him to change, and to decide he wanted

to be free and choose whatever films he wanted. When Metro took exception to this, Gokool took down the Metro symbol – the lion – and replaced it with a globe. He must have felt the bad-tempered lion wasn't going to prevent him from having a global outlook – a free choice. The building has a distinctive three-storey square tower with a low-pitched, overhanging roof and sharply defined eaves supported at each corner by wide, curvilinear brackets, the whole suggestive of an Oriental pavilion. At the same time, art deco neo-classicism asserts itself in the use of traditional round arches, boldly defined on two façades of the tower itself, and symmetrically arranged for the windows of the wings flanking the tower to the west and south.

Over the years, the building has occasionally been the venue of live shows, mainly of local performers: among them was the Trinidad All Steel Percussion Orchestra (TASPO), which performed here on 19 June 1951, a month before appearing at the Festival of Britain, in London. This was a milestone in the history of the steelband. The most famous international musician to perform at the Globe, in July 1941, was the then 25-year-old violinist Yehudi Menuhin. A headline in the *Trinidad Guardian* at the time highlighted a solution to a potential problem for the performance: 'Greased rails for tram-cars on night Menuhin will play.' Apparently, the squeaks of the trams that ran in front of the Globe could be heard inside the building. The clang of the tram bells was also prohibited for that night's performance.

The Church of the Holy Rosary

A Catholic chapel was originally built on this site at the corner of Park and Henry Streets in 1867, and Mass was first celebrated in the small stone building, which seated 150, on 4 May of that year. Twenty-five years later, in 1892, the foundation stone for the church as it exists today was laid. Designed by a Venezuelan architect, José María Hernández, the new building was constructed over a period of 47 years (its two towers were not completed until 1939), although it was used during that time as different parts were added, such as the apse in 1893.

The church is Port of Spain's most outstanding example of late Victorian *Gothic* architecture. Its white-lacquered, *ribbed-vaulted* ceilings rise to 15.2 metres (50 feet), and it contains an impressive collection of stained-glass windows, which were created in Toulouse and installed at its opening. Memorial plaques written in French honour the contributions of French Creole parishioners who lived on nearby streets from the earliest days of the church.

The Church of the Holy Rosary today

St Joseph's Convent

St Joseph's Convent was the first denominational secondary school in Trinidad. It was opened on 1 March 1836, having been founded by the 'Ladies of St Joseph', an order of nuns that had been established 29 years earlier in France. The convent was the first mission of this order in the British West Indies (sister convents had already been established in the French Caribbean, as they were later in St Joseph, San Fernando, Arima and Scarborough in Trinidad and Tobago; and in Dominica, St Lucia, St Vincent and Grenada). Originally located in a large private house one block over on St James (now Frederick) Street, the convent moved to this site on Pembroke (then Kent) Street very shortly after its establishment. Catering largely to the French Creole elite of the time, classes were given mainly in French until around 1870, when the British colonial authorities required the use of English. By then, the convent had an enrolment of 97 girls. Still considered one of the leading schools in the country, the convent now has almost 1000 students.

Centenary Hall, pictured here, is the oldest building now on the convent grounds. Opened in 1907, it commemorates the

Centenary Hall

hundredth anniversary of the founding of the order of the Sisters of Cluny (the formal name for the 'Ladies of St Joseph'), and replaced the residence of the Archbishop of Port of Spain, who lived on this spot for almost 30 years, until 1904. (The archbishop's house had itself replaced the St George's College building on this site, a precursor, then first home, of St Mary's College: that building had served as a Catholic educational institution from 1836 to 1875.) The more modern main block farther north was completed – as was the convent chapel, which faces Abercromby Street – in 1947; it was built after a fire in 1944 had destroyed many of the school's buildings and claimed the lives of four nuns.

The main block of the convent

St Mary's College

Generally considered to be the country's leading Catholic boys' school, St Mary's College (less commonly called the College of the Immaculate Conception) was founded in 1863 by the Holy Ghost Fathers, a French missionary order established in 1703. The college is across the street from the country's leading Catholic girls' school, St Joseph's Convent. St Mary's was, in fact, the second Catholic boys' college to be established in Trinidad: the first, St George's, had been founded in 1836, close by on Cumberland (now Abercromby) Street but, by 1863, had ceased to be a viable institution.

St Mary's was based exclusively in the old St George's building in its opening years, from 1863 to 1866, and moved out of it completely only in 1875. St Mary's initially served the French Creole elite, with classes taught mainly in French during its first seven years until 1870, when the British colonial government required the use of English.

The first building on the present site (an east–west wing) was constructed in 1866 on a plot of land purchased from Eugène Lange. This building no longer exists. Neither do any of the other original buildings constructed in the course of the nineteenth century as the college

The central block of St Mary's College from Frederick Street

purchased adjoining properties. The concrete, cream-coloured central block and chapel shown here were designed by Maurice Acanne, a local architect, and opened in 1943. The twin-towered chapel with its high central steeple has been described by local architect and alumnus Anthony Lewis as 'pseudo-Gothic modern', while the unembellished three-storey central block is surmounted by a simple parapet and a square, flat-topped clock tower. The old college chapel, a prefabricated iron structure, had been on this spot since 1875; its marble altar, a gift of alumni in 1882, still serves as the main altar in today's chapel. The oldest building now on the school property is the wing that runs south of the central block (built in 1925), while the newest is the Father Graf Wing, on Pembroke Street, opened in 1999. It was named after the college's longest-serving teacher and administrator, Leonard Graf, who came to the college in 1905 and retired in 1966, four years before he died. When the college opened, in 1863, it had six day pupils and eight boarders. Today it has just over 1000 students.

The St Mary's College chapel

The Port of Spain State Prison

Known for a century and a half as the Royal Gaol, the Port of Spain State Prison is one of the oldest buildings in the city. It was built in 1812 in the wake of the great fire of 1808. Among many other buildings, the fire destroyed an older prison, located on the west side of George Street, between Queen and Prince Streets, opposite to the city's main market (which is now located on the Beetham Highway). The governor of the time, William Munro, had the new prison built in the upper part of Clarence (today's Frederick) Street, in what was then considered an outlying area of the town.

Port of Spain General Hospital

Pictured here is the oldest part of the Port of Spain General Hospital, which dates back to 1858 and was designed by Lewis Samuels. Known in its earlier days as the Colonial Hospital, it is built on the site of former British military barracks called Orange Grove. Because of this, today's Gordon Street, which leads directly from this building, was known as Barrack Street until the name was changd in 1902. The two-storey building is *Georgian* in style, with the straight line of its front elevation punctuated by Palladian arches on the first floor and tall rectangular windows on the second that almost touch the *balustrade* that runs the length of the flat roof. The arches and windows are all symmetrically arranged one above the other and separated by regularly spaced neo-classical columns and *pilasters* of the Doric and Ionic *orders*.

St Ann's Church of Scotland

The original church on this site was built in 1854 by Presbyterian Portuguese who had first come to Trinidad in 1846 fleeing religious persecution in Madeira. It was first called the United Free Church, then St Ann's Church of Scotland because of its location on St Ann's Road (now Charlotte Street). It was popularly known, however, as the Portuguese Church or Portuguese Chapel because of the background of its congregation, who conducted services for the first 20 years of the church's existence in their native language. Most of this congregation eventually either emigrated to the United States (for example, to Jacksonville, Illinois), or became Catholic through intermarriage with Portuguese and other local Catholics.

The church was rebuilt in 1894 by George Brown in late Victorian *Gothic Revival* style and now serves a Presbyterian congregation that reflects Port of Spain's multi-ethnic population.

Lapeyrouse Cemetery

Lapeyrouse Cemetery is on part of an old sugar estate established by Picot de Lapeyrouse shortly after he arrived in Trinidad from Grenada. He came here under what is known as the 'Cedula of Population' of 1783, an agreement between France and Spain to colonise Trinidad. By the time the British invaded Trinidad in 1797, he had donated almost 4 hectares (9 acres) of the estate to be used as a *campo santo*, or ground for Christian burial, and the cemetery now contains both simple gravesites and elaborate monuments commemorating the dead of the country's diverse population. Traditionally, Protestants were buried in the northern half of the cemetery and Catholics in the southern half, but this is no longer the case. Notable mausoleums are those of the de Verteuil, Gokool, Gordon, and Siegert families. The main entrance arch on Philip Street bears the date of 1869 and was built during the mayoralty of Michel Maxwell Philip, a prominent barrister and legislator.

The Haji Gokool Meah mausoleum

The de Verteuil Mausoleum in Lapeyrouse Cemetery

5 Newtown

St Patrick's Church

The foundation stone for the original Catholic church on this site was laid in 1858. Its construction reflected the expansion westward of Port of Spain in the mid- nineteenth century – creating Newtown in this area – and the need for an additional place of worship for the largely Catholic population of the town. (The only other Catholic church at the time was the cathedral downtown.) A larger-than-life-size statue of St Patrick stands in an ornamented niche above the main door. It is the only flourish on the front elevation of this fairly modest early Victorian *Gothic Revival* church, with its plain pointed arch entranceway and windows, and its separate, rustic belltower with a single exposed bell.

Jenny's

Now a restaurant and bar, Jenny's at 6 Cipriani Boulevard was for over a hundred years the hereditary home of the Boos family. Karl George Boos came to Trinidad from Germany in 1873 at the age of 20 and by 1883 he had become prosperous enough to purchase a plot on the newly developing Tranquillity lands, formerly one of Port of Spain's earliest sugar estates. Boos then hired George Brown, who had just arrived in Trinidad from Scotland to work as an architect and builder, to construct his new home on this site. This was Brown's first project in Trinidad, completed 12 years before he established himself as the island's architect and builder.

The brick and concrete building has an imposing front elevation with its projecting central entranceway, flanked by high wooden galleries on both the lower and upper floors; the roof is capped by two *dormers* symmetrically placed on either side of a square *lantern*, a raised structure to let in additional light and ventilation. Brown was later to make these lanterns a signature feature – in glass and cast iron – of his work, especially in his commercial buildings in downtown Port of Spain. Slender *finials* atop the entranceway, dormers, and lanterns accentuate the verticality of the whole, while a strip of decorative cast iron highlights the ridge of the main roof. Notably missing is *fretwork*, which was to become characteristic of Brown's other houses such as the still extant 'Simpson House' at 6 Queen's Park West.

6 Queen's Park Savannah Area (South)

Queen's Park Savannah

The 219-acre Queen's Park Savannah is today the main recreation park in Port of Spain. Throughout each day, but especially in the mornings and evenings, scores of people can be seen walking, running or jogging along the pitch walk that circles it, and sometimes on the green. In the later eighteenth century, the area was a sugar estate known as Paradise and belonged to the Peschiers, a French Creole family who had come to Trinidad under the Cedula of Population of 1783. The 'Cedula' opened up the island to planters and their slaves from the French islands. In the British days Governor Sir Ralph Woodford purchased the estate (1817), but the Peschiers retained the right, which they hold to this day, to bury family members in a small, walled cemetery in the middle of the former estate. The Savannah was officially named the Queen's Park when Queen Victoria ascended the throne, but people were accustomed to the native name 'savannah' for a grassy

field, and called it 'the Queen's Park Savannah'. The Queen's Park Savannah was initially used mainly as a cow pasture, but in the course of the nineteenth century the park became a centre for a variety of recreational activities and sports, both casual and formal. The first recorded horse race took place in the park in 1828 and the first Grand Stand was erected at the southern end of the park in 1853, facing what was the country's major horse-racing track until 1994. Over the years golf, polo, field hockey, and, of course, cricket and soccer have been played in the Savannah, and on windy days, especially in the dry season of the first half of the year, it is a favourite venue for kite flying. Early in the dry season also, in February or March, the Grand Stand and its immediate surroundings become the site of the main official shows of Carnival, including the steelband contest known as Panorama, the King and Queen of the Bands competitions, and the spectacular parade of bands on the final, and climactic, Monday and Tuesday of the Carnival season. The annual Independence Day Parade is also held at the Savannah on 31 August.

The sidewalk that runs around the perimeter of the park, very popular with casual strollers and joggers, has been traditionally known as the 'Pitch Walk'. For 48 years, from 1902 to 1950, an electric tram track, known as the 'Belt Line', ran alongside the Pitch Walk, between the sidewalk itself and the green grass of the Savannah.

Simpson House

Located at the top of Victoria Avenue on the south side of the Queen's Park Savannah, this single-storey house was designed and built in 1888 for the Siegert family (of Angostura bitters fame) by George Brown. Over the ensuing years it was also owned by the Prada family and by Kenneth Simpson, who married one of Brown's daughters. It is now the office of an architectural firm.

The building has all the hallmarks of Brown's tropical city house design: *fretwork* and *finials* decorating the high *gables*, a *porte cochère*, cast-iron boundary railings and decorative strips along the ridges of the roof, and a *lantern* roof over the dining room for light and ventilation. Also characteristic of his style, but unusual for Port of Spain houses, the building has a cellar.

BP Headquarters/Queen's Park Hotel

The central block of the headquarters of BP Trinidad and Tobago is a faithful replica of the façade of the then new part – the concrete part – of the Queen's Park Hotel, which was built by Tookie Collins in 1937. The original building, which was built in 1895, was torn down along with the Tookie Collins section in 1996. (Incidentally, that graceful-looking original wooden building was completed just before electricity was introduced to Trinidad. It was opened on 16 January 1895, and electricity lit downtown Port of Spain on 5 March that year. The first residence to get the magic light was of course Governor's House, but the second was – yes – the Queen's Park

The headquarters building of BP Trinidad and Tobago

Hotel.) And who was the biggest investor in the newly built hotel? The man who had set up the electric works and who introduced electricity to Trinidad as a project of the Borough Council of Port of Spain. An early advertisement for the original hotel described it as 'the finest situated hotel in the West Indies' and, as late as the 1990s, some of the original structure remained. The replica of the façade of this five-storey block retains the main features of the original *art deco* building: the central curved balconies (now glassed in), on either side of which rise two sleek, ribbed shafts (gently curved at the roof line), punctuated on each floor with rectangular windows decorated with a distinctive raised sun-burst pattern.

The original Queen's Park Hotel

Knowsley

This grand house, which occupies an entire block on the south side of the Queen's Park Savannah, was built in 1906 for William Gordon Gordon, a prominent, Scottish-born local merchant and one of the founders of Gordon Grant and Company. The building was purchased by the government of Trinidad and Tobago in 1956 and now houses the Ministry of Foreign Affairs.

The building is made mainly of imported bricks and local limestone, with marble used in the ground floor gallery. Notable also on the ground floor are double columns supporting rounded arches and a *porte cochère* with dressed grey stonework defining the curves of the arches. The front elevation presents three distinct faces on the upper floors: a high central block with a faux, *half-timbered* high *gable*, flanked on one side by a two-storeyed peppercorn (conical) tower and on the other by a low tower with a stone parapet. The main staircase in the interior is made of purpleheart wood imported from Guyana (British Guiana at the time), and the *gesso* work on the ceiling is by the same Italian craftsman who did similar work in the council chamber of the Red House, the assembly hall of Queen's Royal College, and at Killarney (Stollmeyer's Castle).

National Museum and Art Gallery

Built to commemorate the Golden Jubilee of Queen Victoria's reign (1887), the National Museum and Art Gallery began as the Victoria Institute in 1892. Over the years it has served a variety of functions: offering classes in areas such as painting, needlework, and basic industrial training for young people and adults; affording space for musical and theatrical presentations; and, most importantly, providing exhibition space for local archaeological discoveries and examples of native rocks, fossils, and stuffed fauna. Outstanding among these in the original collection was a comprehensive assemblage of indigenous birds donated by Dr Antoine Léotaud, a local physician and ornithologist.

The institute was extended and renovated in 1902 and, most notably, in 1913, when the Marie Louise Hall was opened in the main building, by then called the King Edward VII Memorial Wing in commemoration of the British monarch, who had died in 1911, two years earlier. Presiding at the opening ceremony was Princess Marie Louise of Schleswig-Holstein herself, Queen Victoria's granddaughter, who announced a new name for the building – the Royal Victoria Institute. Unfortunately, a fire gutted the building in 1920, destroying

its valuable collections. It was, however, quickly rebuilt, in 1923, using the original design. The institute was renamed the National Museum and Art Gallery in 1965 after President's House had served that function for three years. It now contains, in addition to exhibitions of indigenous fauna, an extensive Amerindian archaeological collection based on the discoveries of one-time curator John Bullbrook; displays on Trinidad and Tobago's geology, history, agriculture, and industries; a gallery devoted exclusively to the work of the country's foremost nineteenth-century painter, Michel Jean Cazabon; and an extensive collection of local twentieth-century art. In the back courtyard can be seen the fountain that survived the Red House fire of 1903. For many years, an anchor, reputedly from one of Columbus's ships when he sailed the south coast of Trinidad in 1498, stood outside of the front entrance.

The original design of this Dutch-gabled building was by Daniel Mienerts Hahn, a German who worked in the Department of Public Works. He was also responsible for two other major public buildings of the turn of the twentieth century, the restoration of the heavily fire-gutted Red House and the design of Queen's Royal College.

The National Museum and Art Gallery is located at the northern end of Frederick Street and faces War Memorial Park.

War Memorial in War Memorial Park

Pictured here is a detail of the impressive War Memorial that Trinidad and Tobago erected in honour of its dead of World War I and World War II. This is situated in what used to be called the 'Small Savannah', bounded by Frederick Street North, Wellington Terrace, St Ann's Road, and Keate Street, and it lies opposite to the National Museum and Art Gallery. The authorities spent years in deciding on the site, on what sort of design was appropriate, and most of all to collect funds so it could order the cenotaph from England. The cenotaph was installed on 28 June 1924, and the Small Savannah given the name 'War Memorial Park'.

7 Queen's Park Savannah Area (West)

All Saints Church

This church is the oldest building on the Queen's Park Savannah. Its foundation stone was laid in 1844 and the building opened on 7 May 1846. Originally, it was a *chapel-of-ease* to Holy Trinity Cathedral. Built of stone from Laventille Hill, the structure's simple lancet windows and buttresses and unfussy interior mark it as an example of unaffected early Victorian *Gothic Revival* church architecture. The font in the church was a gift of William Gordon Gordon, a wealthy merchant born in Scotland and the owner of Knowsley. The reredos, a stone and marble ornamental screen at the back of the altar, was installed in 1923, a gift to the church in memory of Gordon Gordon from his widow.

The Gingerbread House

Popularly known as 'the Gingerbread House', this confection of a building was built for Charles Boissière in 1904, the same year that Queen's Royal College and all but one of the other baronial mansions were being built on Maraval Road. It features numerous fanciful *finials*, cast-iron boundary railings and roof ridging, and – perhaps most striking of all – intricate, lace-like *fretwork* along the eaves and especially in the gable bargeboard of the large central *dormer* in the steeply pitched slate roof. On its northern side, an Oriental pavilion – attached and originally a study – features *art nouveau* stained glass. A wide veranda runs along the front of the house,

capped at the southern end by a low conical roof. In his book *Ajoupa*, architect John Newel-Lewis says of it: 'light and air were filtered through the eaves, the *fretwork*, the hanging plants, the galleries, the jalousies, windows and flowing curtains. The sunshine was reduced to a soft glow ….'

The 'Magnificent Seven' Buildings

The first series of landmarks to greet the twentieth century in Port of Spain came with the transfer of a government dairy and stock farm from the former St Clair sugar estate in north-west Port of Spain to Valsayn, about 4 miles to the east. The farm was removed in 1899, opening up this area for housing development. Especially attractive was the stretch along Maraval Road opposite the western face of the Queen's Park Savannah.

In early 1902, seven building plots were laid out along this stretch. Three of the seven lots were allocated to public institutions, and the other four were auctioned for private use. The government reserved the southernmost plot of land for a secondary school. The next one north was allocated to the Anglican Church for an official residence for its bishop. A plot farther north was reserved for an official residence of the Roman Catholic archbishop. All of the other plots were auctioned and they attracted wealthy buyers. The grand houses that were built on them (all but one in 1904) established St Clair for many years as the most exclusive residential area of Port of Spain.

Queen's Royal College

One of the country's major boys' schools, Queen's Royal College (QRC) was opened at this site at Queen's Park West on 25 March 1904. Its predecessor was the Queen's Collegiate School, which was inaugurated almost fifty years earlier, in 1859, at the corner of Cumberland (now Abercromby) and Oxford Streets, facing

Queen's Royal College

Belliard's Orchard (today's Lord Harris Square). Queen's Collegiate was closed in favour of a secondary school where students could take the annual Cambridge examinations, but it was closed more so because Catholic students did not support it yet complained the ruling Anglicans were spending taxpayers' money on Anglican education only. The government announced it was opening a secondary school for all – a school which would be called the Royal College of Trinidad – and said it wanted Catholic support. It asked Queen Victoria for her sponsorship, and on approval they decided to change the name of the Royal College of Trinidad to Queen's Royal College. The College was opened in the Prince's Building in 1870, and was inaugurated in its present building on 24 March 1904.

The main block was designed by a German architect, Daniel Meinerts Hahn, who worked in the Department of Public Works and was also responsible for two other major public buildings – the present Red

Prince's Building was built in 1861 for the visit of Prince Albert. It housed the Queen's Collegiate School from 1870 to 1904 and served as the Town Hall from 1948 to 1961

House and the design of the Royal Victoria Institute. QRC originally contained six classrooms to accommodate 180 students and an auditorium that could seat 550. The college's most distinguishing feature is its 28.25-metre (93-foot) high central tower with a *cornice* about three-quarters of the way up. Directly above the cornice is a clock, originally known as the Edward VII memorial clock, which was added in 1913. A small obelisk commemorating alumni in the Royal Air Force who died in wartime stands directly in front of the tower.

The double-arched second-floor windows of the college, its colourful buff- and blue-grey limestone facings, and ornate *dormers* and *finials* led a prominent local architect, the late John Newel-Lewis, to describe the original central building of the college as 'Venetian and Renaissance' in inspiration. Less distinguished are the three buildings that were added over the years: the science block in 1939, the north block a year later, and the west block in 1956. The Geddes Grant sports pavilion, on the school sports grounds west of the main block, was opened in 1929.

QRC boasts many distinguished alumni, including Dr Eric Williams, the nationalist leader who led the country to independence in 1962; the Nobel Laureate V. S. Naipaul, who once described the main block as 'Italianate'; the writer C. L. R. James, who talks about his experiences at QRC in his famous work on cricket, *Beyond a Boundary*; and Peter Minshall, the renowned designer and Carnival bandleader.

Hayes Court

This is the residence of the Anglican Bishop of Trinidad and Tobago. It was designed and built by George Brown in 1910 and named after Thomas Hayes, Bishop of Trinidad from 1889 until his death in 1904. Hayes Court has served continuously as an episcopal residence since it was first built, apart from a brief period during the tenure of Bishop Arthur Anstey, who rented it to the French consul in order to raise money for church schools.

Hayes Court is much more subdued than its neighbouring buildings along Maraval Road, but it is an impressive structure nonetheless, with its high gables, grey *quoins* for accent, and typical George Brown touches in the use of cast iron in the pillars and railings of the lower gallery and along the ridge of the roof.

Milles Fleurs

Built in 1904 for the Pradas, a Venezuelan-Trinidadian family, this is another creation of George Brown, the Scottish architect who was responsible for most of Port of Spain's finest buildings after the great fire of 1895. Dr Enrique Prada was a prominent public figure, becoming the first mayor of Port of Spain when it was granted city status in 1914. He and his family lived here until 1933, when they sold the house to Joseph Salvatori. The house remained in the Salvatori family until 1973. It was then bought by George Matouk and subsequently by the government of Trinidad and Tobago.

The front elevation, encircled by a wide veranda on the first floor, has three distinct parts on the upper floors: a two-storey round tower with a pepperpot (conical) roof on the southern side; a central gabled block directly above the *porte cochère* of the main entrance; and, to the north, a hexagonal protrusion crowned with an ornate cast-iron *balustrade*. This being a George Brown building, cast iron appears elsewhere as well: in the slender columns of the porte cochère and veranda, and in the railings of the upper balcony and boundaries of the property. A fountain with two figures stands at the centre of the circular front driveway.

Roomor

A prosperous cacao merchant, Lucien F. Ambard, built this extraordinary residence in 1904. He and his family lived there until 1919, when his large mortgage was foreclosed. The house was then purchased by Pointz Mckenzie, who, in turn, also went bankrupt and lost the house in 1923. From 1925 to 1940 it was rented by William Pettigrew Humphrey of Gordon Grant and Company, which held the mortgage. Humphrey was a cinema pioneer in Trinidad and built the *art deco* De Luxe, on Keate Street. When he left the house, it was purchased by another cinema magnate, Timothy Roodal, a former mayor of San Fernando. The house remains in the Roodal family to this day, but is now called Roomor, syllables of Roodal and Morgan. (Morgan is the husband of Roodal's daughter, who has inherited the house.)

The building has been generally described as 'French Baroque' in style, but its flamboyant architectural features are not easily categorised. John Newel-Lewis, architect, characterised it as a 'queen of architecture', adding, 'The crowning glory of this great house is in its roof, whose towers, pinnacles, dormers and copulas of unusual proportions, together with its roof galleries, form a skyline unusual in these parts.'

Archbishop's House

The Roman Catholic Archbishop's Residence on Maraval Road was built, like its neighbours, in 1904. Previously, the archbishop had lived for almost 30 years in a residence on the grounds of St Joseph's Convent, on Pembroke Street. Archbishop Patrick Flood was the first resident of the building and the street immediately to the south of this house is named in his honour.

Constructed by George Brown, whose own designs are evident elsewhere in Port of Spain, this palatial structure of red granite was conceived in Ireland by an Irish architect, who, it has been said, was under the influence of Eastern as well as Western forms (Archbishop Flood himself is also said to have influenced the design). The tower and its turret, which is the most striking feature of the residence, have a distinctly early medieval, or *Romanesque*, appearance with their *crenellated* parapets and round arches and *loopholes*. The round arches continue in the upper and lower galleries, which are deeply recessed, suggesting to some a cloister (though one turned inside out!), to others the wide shaded veranda of an Eastern palace. Eastern influences have also been noted in the decorative open medallions above the arches on the first floor.

Imported marble and local cedar and greenheart wood are used extensively in the interior of the residence, which contains the archbishop's and other offices, a reception hall, and a dining room on the ground floor; and four bedrooms and a private drawing room on the second floor. During the long tenure of Archbishop Dowling (1907–1940), a French Dominican priest with leprosy was quarantined until his death in the third-floor room of the tower. The small chapel adjacent to the main building is dedicated to St Clare.

Whitehall

Whitehall, the office of the prime minister of Trinidad and Tobago, is the largest of the private mansions constructed in 1904 along Maraval Road. It was built by Joseph Léon Agostini, a wealthy, Corsican-born cacao planter who came to Trinidad as a child. Agostini actually had the building painted rose-pink originally and called it Rosenweg (German for 'the Way of the Roses'). When he died suddenly in 1906, the heavily mortgaged home had to be sold by his family. It was purchased by Robert Henderson, who then had it painted white and gave it the name it has today. The Henderson family occupied Whitehall for the next 33 years, from 1907 to 1940, when they vacated it to accommodate the administrative offices of the American forces that were based in Trinidad during the war. The Americans occupied it until 1944, when it was leased to the British Council. For the next ten years, it served as an active cultural centre, giving rise to a vibrant drama company, the Whitehall Players, and serving as the home of the Trinidad Art Society, the Cellar Club, the Trinidad Central Library, and the Government Broadcasting Unit. The Government of Trinidad and Tobago bought it in 1954 and it served briefly, in 1957, as the headquarters of the interim government of the short-lived Federation of the West Indies. Subsequently it has served on two occasions as the office of the prime minister, from 1961 to 1986

and from 1999 to the present. Whitehall has also been featured on the screen: it was portrayed as Government House in the 2002 film of V. S. Naipaul's novel *The Mystic Masseur*.

The main building material of Whitehall is coral from Barbados, which John Newel-Lewis, the late architect, described as giving the impression of being carved in a single block to produce the rectangular three-storeyed front elevation of the structure. The entrance way, the approach to which is watched over by two bronze sentinels, is spanned by Moorish *arches*, which are echoed in the three recessed windows directly above, on the second floor. A *balustrade* appears above the third-floor attic, and this surrounds a rooftop terrace, on which stands a pavilion (traditionally known as the Blue Room), which originally had two towers, one at its northern end and one at its southern. The overall exterior effect is that of a Venetian palazzo.

The interior of the building, now extensively reconfigured to accommodate government offices, once contained reception rooms, a library, and a large living room and drawing room on the first floor (the last decorated in Wedgwood blue); six bedroom suites on the second floor; and, unusual for a Port of Spain building, a basement (extensive enough to contain a kitchen and pantry, serving rooms, a breakfast room, and a wine cellar).

Stollmeyer's Castle (Killarney)

Built in 1904, like most of the other mansions along this northern stretch of Maraval Road, this building is called Killarney or, more popularly, Stollmeyer's Castle. It is named after its original owner, Charles Fourier Stollmeyer, a second-generation German-Trinidadian who was a pioneer of the asphalt industry on the island. He never lived in Stollmeyer's Castle, but gave it to his son, Charles Conrad, as a wedding present. Charles Conrad resided there for over 60 years, until 1965. The family sold it in 1972 and it was eventually acquired by the government of Trinidad and Tobago, which now owns it.

Stollmeyer's Castle was designed by the Scottish architect Robert Gillies and built by the local firm of Taylor and Gillies (Taylor was a son-in-law of Charles Fourier Stollmeyer). It is built of imported pale-yellow brick trimmed with blue-grey local limestone from Laventille Hill, in east Port of Spain, and the open galleries on the ground floor have floors of Italian marble and cast-iron pillars topped with a horse motif (an echo of the horse weather vane at the pinnacle of the Balmoral-style *turret* and tower). The second-floor front window of the square central tower has an *art nouveau* decorative panel and at the base of the tower stands a *porte cochère*, surmounted, like the tower itself, by a stone parapet. Two *gables* flank the tower, one facing the front directly; the other, facing the north-east at an angle, is stepped in the Dutch manner. The original interior of the building had five joined reception rooms and six bedrooms, with purpleheart wood from Guyana used extensively for the floors and staircases, mahogany for doors, *wainscoting*, and doorway and window frame mouldings.

8 Queen's Park Savannah Area (North)

President's House

Once known as Government House, President's House is the official residence of the president of the Republic of Trinidad and Tobago. Located at the eastern end of the Botanic Gardens on land that was once part of the Hollandais estate, this mansion was built between 1873 and 1876. It was the fifth of the official governor's residences.

The first governor to live in this new residence was Sir Henry Turner Irving, and

he was succeeded over the next 84 years by 19 British-born governors. The first non-British head of state, Jamaica-born Governor-General Sir Solomon Hochoy, lived here for eight years (1965 to1973). The mansion had actually already been renamed Governor-General's House in 1958, when it became the residence of the first (and only) governor-general of the Federation of the West Indies.

The house was designed by a Mr Ferguson, and is built of local blue limestone from the Picadilly and Laventille quarries in south-east Port of Spain. It is commonly described as being of 'Indian colonial' style and presents three distinct parts from the front: a western wing with a *hipped roof* and arched gallery; a central block that has a gabled roof with *dormers*, and open galleries on both storeys with cast-iron columns and filigreed railings; and a tower-like eastern wing with a stone *parapet*. All the roofs are covered in slate. Inside, the house has a grand staircase and notable public rooms including the Long Room and the Great Hall, which can seat about 200 and are used for diplomatic receptions and events such as national awards ceremonies. The low building with a former clock tower just beside the residence pre-dates President's House and originally contained stables.

The Botanic Gardens

The Botanic Gardens in Port of Spain, nearly two hundred years old, lie just to the north of the Queen's Park Savannah and cover 28 hectares (70 acres). Most of this land was originally part of Hollandais Estate, which was purchased by the colonial government in 1819. The gardens themselves, originally known as the Royal Botanic Gardens, were laid out in 1820 at the direction of the governor, Sir Ralph Woodford. Under his direction also, the Nutmeg Ravine, of which evidence still remains, was created to divert water from the St Ann's River to provide irrigation for the gardens. It ran in an east–west direction across the gardens, through the north-west section of the Queen's Park Savannah, then, crossing the road to Maraval, flowed through lands of what became the St Clair Estate, to empty itself in the Maraval River. The gardens have an impressive variety of tropical trees and plants, both native and imported: they contain an estimated 870 species of trees (including balata, poui, and immortelle), as well as many types of ferns, shrubs, and herbaceous ornamentals. The first curator, David Lockhart, is buried in a small cemetery in the gardens, as are a number of other prominent public figures, including Governor George Fitzgerald Hill, who presided over Emancipation and the abolition of slavery, Charles William Warner, a powerful nineteenth-century attorney-general of Trinidad, and Sir Solomon Hochoy, the first Caribbean-born governor and governor-general of Trinidad and Tobago.

No longer existing in the gardens but worthy of note was 'The Cottage', pictured below, which was the residence of the governor for nine years, between 1867 and 1876, the year in which the new Government House (now President's) was opened. This building had originally been an estate manager's house and it survived until 1886. The English writer Charles Kingsley stayed there in late 1869 to early 1870 on a visit that resulted in his book *At Last! A Christmas in the West Indies*. An entire chapter in that book is devoted to the rich variety of plant and animal life – in Kingsley's own words, 'a multitude of sights and sounds so utterly new and strange' – that he observed around him during his stay in the gardens. The Cottage was located at the western end of the gardens, close to the entrance of the small Emperor Valley Zoo (which opened in 1952).

The Botanic Gardens

Gordon's Cottage

The Hollow

This is the Hollow, the name given to a landscaped depression at the north-western end of the Queen's Park Savannah. The Hollow is what remains of a reservoir dug in 1851 at the request of Governor Lord Harris (1846 to 1854), in an effort to bring piped water into the centre of Port of Spain. The water to supply the reservoir came from the Nutmeg Ravine, which watered the Botanic Gardens just to the north and continued to the west along what is now Serpentine Road to empty into the Maraval River. The Hollow also figures prominently in Trinidad and Tobago's aviation history. The first flight ever in the country ended tragically here on 23 January 1913, when a visiting American aviator, Frank Boland, attempted to give an exhibition here. He took off in his single-seater biplane just east of the Grand Stand, at the southern end of the Savannah, gaining an altitude of 30 metres. Minutes later he crashed and was killed in this area.

Belmont Hill/Trinidad Hilton

The modern, 400-room Trinidad Hilton Hotel, which dominates Belmont Hill, just to the north-east of the Queen's Park Savannah, was opened in 1962. Popularly known as 'the upside-down hotel' because the lobby in the main block is at the top of the building, it sits on the site of a house that was home to three of the governors of Trinidad: Sir Thomas Hislop (1803–11), Sir William Munro (1811–13), and Sir Ralph Woodford (1813–28). The property upon which the house was situated was leased to the government by the Barry family. This family wished to terminate the tenancy of Woodford and the matter went before the Privy Council twice, and in the end Woodford had to leave. He could not have been too upset though, for he himself said of the house: 'It was neither wind nor water-tight, there being scarcely a dry spot during heavy rains.' He had named the house 'Belmont', which itself gave its name to a pasture not far to the south of it. Later, slaves moving towards that area called their settlement after the nearby pasture – 'Belmont'. It was owing to his search for a new place that Woodford found the Hollandais estate house, which he renovated as a cottage and made his home.

Queen's Hall

Queen's Hall is located on a hectare and a half (3 ½ acres) of land in St Ann's, just to the east of President's House and to the south of the prime minister's residence. Since its opening in 1959 it has been the home of concerts, operas, recitals, dance, festivals and other live entertainments. The building also figured prominently in Trinidad and Tobago's build-up to independence – an important draft constitution conference took place there in April 1962 and, on the eve of Independence Day itself, 30 August of the same year, it was the venue for a celebratory gala performance of some 700 performers from all over the country. This took place in the presence of Her Royal Highness the Princess Royal, who had come to open Trinidad and Tobago's first parliament; the governor-general, Sir Solomon Hochoy; the prime minister designate Dr Eric Williams; and other dignitaries.

Designed by local architect Colin Laird, who also designed the National Library, the Hasely Crawford Stadium, and the Brian Lara Promenade, it was intended originally as a multi-purpose building, something of a grand community centre that would accommodate not just stage performances but also a wide variety of events such as art shows, lectures, and even sports like basketball. Over the years, however, the use of the space was increasingly limited to stage presentations. The building was extensively renovated in 2002, when its original 1250 seats were reduced to 840.

9 Port of Spain West

Queen's Park Oval

Located in the St Clair district, the Queen's Park Oval is one of the world's major cricket grounds. In his autobiography, *Long Innings*, the famous cricketer Sir Pelham Warner, described the Oval as 'one of the most beautiful in the world'. In addition to Warner himself, who was born in Port of Spain, the grounds evoke the names of star players like Lebrun Constantine, Learie Constantine, Gerry Gomez, Andy Ganteaume, Frank Worrell, Garfield Sobers, Len Hutton, Neil Harvey, Sonny Ramadhin, Allan Border and Brian Lara. Since 1891, when the Queen's Park Cricket Club was founded, it has dominated the sport locally, including the running of the Oval. The club came to this site in 1896, after being based for five years in

the Queen's Park Savannah. It was called then the Sovereign Cricket Club. The land on which the Oval is built was originally part of a government dairy and stock farm that had been established in 1884 on the abandoned St Clair sugar estate and which, by 1899, had been completely sold off, mainly for private housing development. The first major match took place here in 1897, when a British team, led by Lord Hawke, played against a local team. It was played on a matting wicket; a turf wicket was not laid down until 1954, in time for the visit of the Australian cricket team. Over the years, the Oval has expanded its capacity and it can now accommodate almost 17,000 spectators in its various stands. These stands are named after famous players such as Learie Constantine and Jeffrey Stollmeyer, and also after some of its benefactors. In addition to cricket, the Oval has over the years accommodated other activities such as soccer and cycling, rallies for visiting British royalty, religious assemblies, Carnival Queen shows, and large outdoor parties. The Oval now also has a gym, as well as squash and tennis courts. In 2004, The Queen's Park Cricket Club, which leases and manages the Oval, agreed to admit women to its membership. This cricket ground and stands are now undergoing renovations for the Cricket World Cup, 2007.

Briar's End

Located at the corner of Sweet Briar Road and Elizabeth Street, Briar's End has been a prominent landmark overlooking the eastern boundary of the Queen's Park Oval since the beginning of the twentieth century, when this area of St Clair was being developed for housing. The area had originally been part of a large sugar estate which had been abandoned then purchased in 1884 by the government for housing development south of St Clair Avenue, where Briar's End is located; and for an experimental dairy and stock farm, north of the avenue, which was eventually also developed for housing when the government moved the farm in 1899. The original estate house, now the site of the 11-storey TATIL building on Maraval Road, was called Sweet Briar House, from which the street and this house gets its name.

This large, flamboyant house, with its wide, canopied bow windows and steep *gables* and *dormers* decorated with intricate *fretwork* and topped with pronounced *finials* like the tips of a ship's masts, has been described by the local artist and city historian Adrian Camps-Campins as 'giving the impression of the flagship of an armada under sail'. This is especially so in its western elevation.

The house was owned by Henry Israel Jeffers and is well known because of its association with Audrey Jeffers, his daughter, one of the pioneers of social welfare in Trinidad and Tobago. She saw service in World War I, and after returning to Trinidad in 1920 she opened a school in his house. Later, she was one of the founders of the Coterie of Social Workers, which still exists today, and whose social work included setting up 'breakfast sheds' to serve meals to under-privileged primary school children in Port of Spain and other towns in the country. Audrey Jeffers was also active in politics and became the first woman elected to the City Council (in 1936) and the first one nominated to the Legislative Council of Trinidad and Tobago (in 1946). For her public service, she received the Order of the British Empire and, at the first post-independence national awards ceremony in 1969, was posthumously awarded the Chaconia Gold Medal. The Port of Spain foreshore highway is named in her honour.

(Former) Roxy Cinema

Now a pizza parlour, this building still bears the name of Roxy, which was its original name when it opened as a cinema in October 1934. It was built by the movie magnate Timothy Roodal, who had been mayor of San Fernando (and who, six years later, was to purchase the mansion on upper Maraval Road now known as Roomor). The building served for over 60 years mainly as a cinema but also as a venue for live performances such as dance shows and the city's annual Christmas pantomime. Its white façade with its double columns of the Corinthian *order* provides Port of Spain's most complete example of twentieth-century neo-classical architecture.

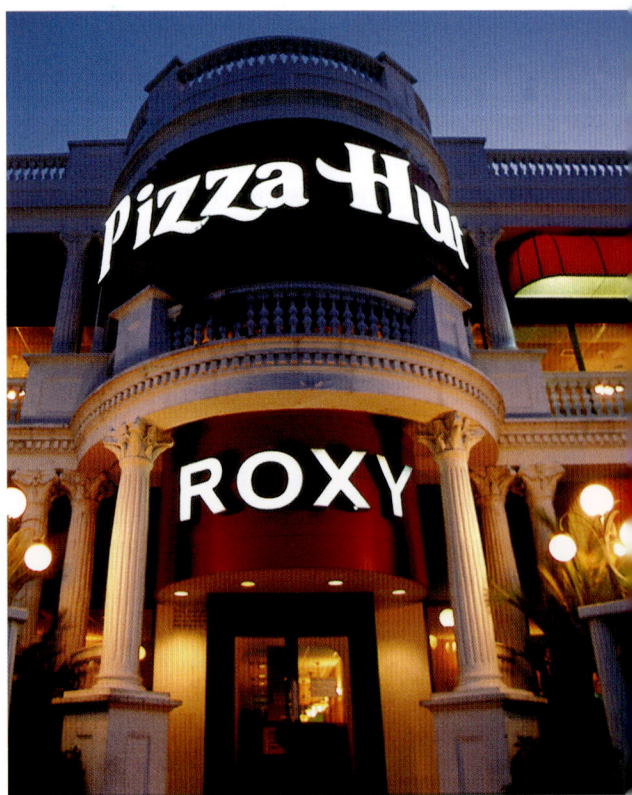

St James Barracks and Police Commissioner's House

The foundation stone of the St James Barracks was laid on 13 May 1824, and the original buildings on this property (originally 57 hectares, or 143 acres) were completed in 1827. The barracks, with accommodation for about 400 men, were built for regiments of the British army, which remained here until 1889. A year later, the buildings were turned into a training school for the local police and, in 1906, they also became the headquarters of the police mounted branch. The original barracks and subsequent buildings still fulfil these two functions. The barracks are fine examples of local *Georgian* architecture, as is the Police Commissioner's House, at the entrance to the barracks complex. It was built at the same time as the barracks. The whole area of western Port of Spain takes its name, St James, from the barracks.

The Police Commissioner's House

Paschim Kaashi Mandir

The Paschim Kaashi (Benares of the West) Mandir, located in a complex on Ethel Street in St James, houses a large main mandir, or temple, four smaller mandirs, and a cultural centre. The complex serves a sizeable Hindu population in St James, an area formerly known as Peru Sugar Estate, where indentured East Indians were settled ever since they began arriving here in 1845 (indentured immigration ended in 1917). St James Barracks were the only neighbours of Peru Estate, which was so cut off and isolated that out of nostalgia the indentured estate workers gave the roadways that emerged – now streets – such names as Benares, Nepaul, Madras, Calcutta, Bengal and Bombay. The Paschim Kaashi Mandir was designed by architect John Newel-Lewis and built in 1962, with expansion in 1970 to allow for additional altars. Its roof is multi-domed, and marble and concrete murtis, or statues, of Hindu deities abound throughout the main mandir, including ones of Sri Krishna, Radha, Siva, Durga, Hanuman and Ganesh; and marble Dashavatars (ten incarnations, or forms) of Lord Vishnu. The four smaller mandirs are devoted to Rama, Siva, Hanuman, and Kali. The lion statues in Kali mandir, as well as the copper mace that crowns the Hanuman mandir, are the work of Ken Morris.

Haji Gokool Meah Memorial Masjid

Located on the Western Main Road in St James, this *masjid* (smaller or local mosque) is named after real estate and cinema entrepreneur Haji Gokool Meah, who financed its building in the late 1920s. Gokool was born in Kashmir and came with his family to Trinidad in 1853 at the age of six as part of the large influx to Trinidad of indentured labour from India after the abolition of slavery. A devout Muslim, he made the pilgrimage, or *haj*, to Mecca in 1922 (hence the title 'Haji'). This almost all-white mosque is rectangular in shape, and its central dome and round, minaret-like columns reflect features of traditional Islamic architecture. The use of green to accentuate the roof line and arched windows of the masjid is also of religious significance as this colour is sacred in the Muslim faith. The building can accommodate around 500 worshippers.

St James Medical Complex

Erected in 1929, these buildings were originally known collectively as the House of Refuge or, more informally, as the Poor House. This institution to house the destitute of Port of Spain had been located farther east until then, in a block bounded by Maraval Road, Gray Street, Tragarete Road, and Alcazar Street (close to St Patrick's Church). The inadequacy of those facilities, as well as the expansion southwards of the housing development of St Clair, led the government to build the institution anew on this land, which had been part of the Terre Brûlée estate. Its building was a major spur in the development of St James: less than ten years later, in 1938, the district was incorporated into Port of Spain. The buildings now house the St James Medical Complex, which offers radiotherapy and geriatric services.

Woodbrook (Mucurapo) Cemetery

Woodbrook Cemetery is Port of Spain's second largest burial ground. Although it has a gravesite dated 1869, the site was not fully established as a cemetery until the early years of the twentieth century, and for many years it was called (and is still known to many locals as) the Mucurapo Cemetery. The name *Mucurapo* is Amerindian in origin, from *Cu-Mucurapo* ('The Place of the Silk Cotton Trees') and the area, close to the shore in western Port of Spain, is of significant historic interest. It was here that the Spanish first attempted to establish a foothold in Trinidad in 1531 with the arrival of Antonio Sedeño and a troop of 70 soldiers. Most of the Spaniards were killed in this attempt but, armed with reinforcements from the mainland across the Gulf of Paria, Sedeño returned twice in the following two years, finally winning the battle of Cu-Mucurapo. It was here also that the British came ashore when they invaded Trinidad in 1797.

Woodbrook Cemetery has few elaborate gravesites. It is known, though, for the monument to Michael (Mikey) Cipriani and

The Cipriani monument

Leslie Bradshaw, the former described on the tombstone as 'the pioneer of local aviation and one of the leading sportsmen in the West Indies'. Mikey Cipriani and Bradshaw took off from the Mucurapo field at 8.10 a.m. on 3 June 1934, headed for Tobago, but crashed shortly afterwards in the mountains of the Northern Range. A local hero, Mikey Cipriani's funeral procession to the cemetery nine days later attracted an estimated 20,000 mourners. Also noteworthy in the north-eastern corner of the cemetery is a Jewish graveyard, consisting mainly of the graves of refugees from Nazi persecution who arrived in Trinidad between 1936 and 1939.

Jewish graves in Woodbrook Cemetery

Hasely Crawford Stadium and Jean Pierre Sports Complex

These are located side by side and close to the Invaders Bay section of Port of Spain. The sporting facility was originally called the National Stadium when it was opened in 1982 but was renamed to honour Hasely Crawford for his 100-metre victory at the Montreal Olympics in 1976. The stadium seats 27,000 patrons. Mainly used for soccer and track-and-field sports, the stadium also accomodates music shows and other large outdoor events.

Hasely Crawford Stadium

The Sports Complex next door to the stadium is named after the country's outstanding netball player, Jean Pierre, who died in 2002. It provides facilities for netball, basketball, badminton, table tennis, tennis, and music concerts. The piece of sculpture that stands outside the complex is by Pat Chu Foon.

Sculpture by Pat Chu Foon outside the Jean Pierre Sports Complex

Fort George

This site, with its magnificent view of Port of Spain and the Gulf of Paria, is located north-west of the city, at 340 metres (1120 feet). When it was first built in 1805, under Governor Sir Thomas Hislop, it was called Fort Vigie (Fort Look-out), but it was soon afterwards renamed for the reigning British king, George III. In charge of constructing both the winding road up the mountain and the fort itself was Jonas Mohammed Bath, an African who had been brought to Trinidad as a slave. (He was also a prominent leader of local Mandingo Africans, who were predominantly Muslim.) While there are still some low walls and cannon from the original fort, the principal building on the site today was actually erected in 1883 as a signal station. It used to receive flag signals regarding ship traffic from the North Post Wireless Station, which overlooked the Caribbean Sea from the head of the Diego Martin Valley just to the west; in turn, the Fort George station would signal (again by flag) the harbourmaster's office in Port of Spain to the south-east. The Fort George station was designed and built by an Ashanti prince, Kofi Nti, who had been brought to Trinidad from West Africa as a ward of the colonial government after the 1873–4 war against his people by the British. While in Trinidad, he was assigned to work in the local Works Department.

Looking east towards Port of Spain from Fort George

10 Maraval

Trinidad Country Club

The Trinidad Country Club is located in the Maraval district, north-west and just outside of Port of Spain proper. It sits on 12 acres of land, a grant made in 1784 to Philippe-Rose Roume de St Laurent, the man responsible for bringing French planters and their slaves to Trinidad. Philippe-Rose, who did not accept the grant, passed it on to his mother, Rose de Gannes de la Cancellerie. She called the estate Champs Elysées, and grew a variety of crops on it, causing Mrs Carmichael, an English writer, to describe it as 'a most agreeable neighbourhood' given to groves of fruit trees 'laden with their treasures', and to forest trees 'of noble growth'.

The Country Club today

A house was first built on the estate in 1780, and in 1815 governor Sir Ralph Woodford expressed interest in buying the property for his residence, but the government did not have enough funds. The original estate house on Champs Elysées was replaced around 1820, and lasted some fifty years, until it was destroyed by fire and was replaced by the building that we see today, with its *crenellated parapet* suggestive of a small French château. In 1904, the property was reduced to its present size when land to the north was given to two de Boissière sons. The de Boissière family owned Champs Elysées until 1932, when it was purchased by the Queens' Park Hotel Co. Ltd., and turned into the Trinidad Country Club, for years an exclusive private institution. When local rum tycoon J. B. Fernandes acquired this company in 1955, he became the proprietor of the club, and it remained in the hands of the Fernandes family until recently.

The Champs Elysées estate at the time of the de Boissière family

Glossary

Arch A structure that forms the upper edge of an open space and supports the weight above it. It is usually pointed or rounded, the former characteristic of Gothic architecture and the latter of Romanesque and Moorish styles. Gothic Revival buildings in Port of Spain – the city's two cathedrals, the Church of the Holy Rosary, All Saints Anglican Church, St Patrick's Church, and St Ann's Church of Scotland – feature pointed arches, as does the newly restored Old Police Headquarters; Romanesque round arches can be seen at the Archbishop's House. A variation of the round arch is the Venetian arch, which is evident in the striking second-floor front windows of Queen's Royal College: it consists of two round arches framed within a larger round arch and separated by a small column, above which is a small circular glass panel. Another notable style of round arch is the Moorish, which is horseshoe-shaped: White Hall has trefoiled (or three-cusped) versions of these. Flat and depressed arches are not as common, though the former dominate the entire front elevation of the downtown Treasury Building. The latter are a major feature of the distinctive façade of the United Brothers Masonic Lodge in east Port of Spain.

Art deco A style of design that was popular in the 1920s and 1930s. Also referred to as the Style Moderne, it is characterised by elegant streamlining and by geometric designs and shapes (such as the chevron). In Port of Spain, the Treasury Building, the restored main block of the former Queen's Park Hotel (now part of the BP headquarters), and the Globe Cinema are the best examples.

Art nouveau A style of design that flourished from about 1890 until about 1914. It is characterised by sinuous, flowing lines and asymmetrical, organic forms such as elongated and intertwining foliage. Stained glass examples of the style can be seen at the Gingerbread House and at Stollmeyer's Castle.

Arts and Crafts Movement A late nineteenth-century aesthetic and social movement that promoted the revival of traditional (mainly medieval) craftsmanship in an age of mass production and industrialization. Its main proponent was the Englishman William Morris (from whom the Morris chair gets its name). In architecture, the movement was closely allied with the later years of the Gothic Revival. The design of Stollmeyer's Castle was influenced by the movement.

Balustrade A row of short pillars joined by a rail or topping of masonry. Balustrades are especially notable when they appear on the roofs of buildings, as they do at the General Hospital, Whitehall, and Milles Fleurs.

Chapel-of-ease A church that is subordinate to and supportive of a main church, as All Saint's Church was originally in relation to Holy Trinity Cathedral.

Crenellated Having alternating upper and lower parts, as in a parapet or the battlements of a castle. The best examples of crenellated parapets in Port of Spain can be seen at the Archbishop's House and the Trinidad Country Club.

Cornice A moulded projection along and at (or near) the top of an internal wall or the exterior of a building or other structure. A striking example in Port of Spain can be seen in the tower of the Main Block of Queen's Royal College, just below the clock.

Dormer A projecting window set in a sloping roof. The most ornate dormers in Port of Spain are those on the roofs of Queen's Royal College and the Gingerbread House.

Elevation An external façade of a building.

Entablature Upper, horizontal part of the exterior of a classical building resting on columns, but also found in classical or classically influenced interior structures such as behind the Speaker's dais in the Legislative Chamber of the Red House.

Finial An ornament at the top of a gable or other high part of a building. Finials abound in the late nineteenth- and early twentieth-century buildings of Port of Spain such as Jenny's, the Simpson House, the Gingerbread House, Queen's Royal College, and Briar's End.

Fretwork Ornamental woodwork done with a fretsaw, especially notable on the exteriors of late nineteenth- and early twentieth-century buildings such as the Gingerbread House, Briar's End, and numerous other private and public buildings in Port of Spain.

Gable The wall section closing the end of a pitched or sloping roof, and usually triangular in shape. The high gable of the Gingerbread House is particularly notable. The National Museum and Art Gallery has examples of Dutch (curved) gables, while Stollmeyer's Castle features prominent triangular and stepped gables.

Georgian The architectural and other styles of the age of the first four King Georges of the United Kingdom (1714–1830). The dominant influence is neo-classicism, with its orderly, unfussy elegance: Georgian buildings of the time featured understatedly adorned window and door openings, *pediments*, sloping roofs hidden behind parapets, and symmetrically arranged *pilasters* and columns. Port of Spain's best examples of the style are the old General Hospital building, the St James Barracks, and the Police Commissioner's House.

Gesso A substance consisting of plaster of Paris (gypsum), glue and ground chalk. It is used to raise a flat surface slightly for decorative purposes. Gesso work can be found in the Legislative Chamber of the Red House, the assembly hall of Queen's Royal College, and at Stollmeyer's Castle and Knowsley, all done in the early years of the twentieth century by the same Italian craftsman.

Gothic Revival A movement in the second half of the eighteenth century and throughout the nineteenth century that encouraged the revival of Gothic, or medieval, architectural forms and features such as pointed-arch windows and doors, stained-glass windows, steeply pitched roofs, and fan vaults. It is most often associated with ecclesiastical and academic buildings. Examples in Port of Spain are the city's two cathedrals, the Church of the Holy Rosary, All Saints Anglican Church, St Patrick's Church, and St Ann's Church of Scotland.

Half-timbering Timber framing of a building in which the framing is left visible on the outside wall, common in English buildings of the Tudor period (late fifteenth and sixteenth centuries). The high gable of the central block of Knowsley has faux half-timbering: the visible timber is not actually part of the framing but is used decoratively.

Hammer-beam A short, bracket-like beam that projects into the upper part of a room from a major rafter. Holy Trinity Cathedral is notable for its hammer-beam mahogany ceiling.

Hipped roof A roof with no gables but with four pitched, or sloping, roofs joined at hips (the angle from the ridge of the roof to the eaves where two slopes meet). The western wing of President's House has such a roof.

Lantern A structure rising above a roof that lets in additional light and ventilation. They are very characteristic of the late nineteenth-century domestic and commercial buildings designed by George Brown, such as Jenny's, the Simpson House, and a number of stores in downtown Port of Spain.

Loophole A narrow vertical opening in a wall for admitting light and air and, in the case of a fortification, for shooting through.

Martello tower A circular tower used for coastal defence. They were built mainly in the early nineteenth century in the United Kingdom during the Napoleonic Wars when there were fears of a French invasion. Port of Spain has one of the few that exist in the Americas: Fort Picton on Laventille Hill, built around 1800.

Order A style of classical or neo-classical column or pilaster, most commonly identified by the type of ornamentation on its capital, or topmost part. The simplest orders are the Doric and Tuscan, while the Ionic, Corinthian, and Composite orders are more elaborate. The Railway Headquarters Building in downtown Port of Spain has examples of Tuscan pilasters. Columns of the Corinthian and Composite orders may be seen on the south-east elevation of the Red House, and the oldest part of the General Hospital has Doric and Ionic columns and pilasters.

Parapet A low wall, usually at the edge of a roof.

Pediment A wide, low-pitched, usually triangular gable, often found over an entranceway or façade in classical and neo-classical buildings. The most prominent examples in Port of Spain can be found on the Red House and Railway Headquarters Building.

Pilaster A column-like shaft attached to a wall. Unlike a column, however, a pilaster is rectangular in shape rather than circular, and it has no structural purpose. Pilasters may be seen on the Railway Headquarters Building and on the oldest part of the General Hospital.

Pitch The angle of the slope of a roof or gable.

Porte cochère Strictly speaking, a large entranceway to a house or courtyard that allows vehicles to enter from the street. Now commonly (if loosely) used to refer to a projecting canopy that is wide enough to allow vehicles to pass though. A number of Port of Spain's buildings, especially those from the late nineteenth and early twentieth centuries, have this feature: for example, the Simpson House, Knowsley, the Gingerbread House, Stollmeyer's Castle, and Milles Fleurs.

Quoin External corner of a structure, especially when it takes the form of dressed, or finished, stone- or brick-work.

Romanesque The dominant architectural style in Western Europe between the seventh and twelfth centuries. Its most notable feature is the round arch. Its influence can be seen in the Archbishop's House.

Rib-vaulting A prominent ceiling arch, such as the one found at the Church of the Holy Rosary, in which each segment of the vault is conspicuously framed at the ribs, or edges.

Turret A small tower, usually part of a bigger structure such as a large tower. Turrets are features of three neighbouring buildings on upper Maraval Road: Roomor, the Archbishop's House, and Stollmeyer's Castle.

Wainscoting Wooden panelling on the lower part of an interior wall.

Bibliography

Alleyne, Garth (ed.). *QRC 2004*. Port of Spain: QRC 2004 Committee, 2004.

Besson, Gerard, and Brereton, Bridget. *The Book of Trinidad*. Port of Spain: Paria Publishing, 1992.

Besson, Gerard. *A Photograph Album of Trinidad at the Turn of the 19th Century*. Port of Spain: Paria Publishing, 1985.

Borde, Pierre Gustave Louis, *The History of Trinidad under the Spanish Government*, vol. I (1498–1622), Paris , Maisonneuve et cie, 1876 (vol. II published 1882). Vol. I translated by James Alva Bain in 1932, vol. II by A. S. Mavrogordato in 1961, both republished by Paria Publishing in 1982

Carmichael, Mrs. *Domestic Manners and Social Conditions of the White, Coloured, and Negro Population in the West Indies*. 2 volumes. Originally published London: Whittaker, Treacher and Co., 1833. Reprinted 1969 New York: Negro Universities Press.

Centenary Record of the Holy Ghost Fathers in Trinidad and of St. Mary's College 1863–1963. Port of Spain: St Mary's College, 1963.

De Verteuil, L. A. A. *Trinidad: Its Geography, Natural Resources, Administration, Present Condition, and Prospects*, 2nd edn. (1st edn. 1856). London/Paris/New York: Cassell, 1884.

James, C. L. R. *Beyond a Boundary*. London: Stanley, 1963.

Kingsley, Charles. *At Last: A Christmas in the West Indies*. London: Macmillan, 1871.

Leigh Fermor, Patrick. *The Traveller's Tree: A Journey Through the Caribbean Islands*. London: John Murray, 1950.

Lewis, John Newel. *Ajoupa*. [Port of Spain] self-published, 1983.

Lewis, John Newel. *Killarney: Stollmeyer's Castle*. Port of Spain: Aquarella Galleries, 1988.

MacLean, Geoffrey. *Cazabon: An Illustrated Biography of Trinidad's Nineteenth Century Painter Michel Jean Cazabon*. Port of Spain: Aquarela Galleries, 1986.

MacLean, Geoffrey. *Cazabon: The Harris Collection*. Port of Spain: MacLean Publishing, 1999.

Mavrogordato, Olga J. *Voices in the Street*. Port of Spain: Paria Publishing, 1996.

Morris, Jan. 'Howzat? And Mr. Morgan: Port of Spain 1958', in *Cities*. London: Faber and Faber, 1963.

Navarro, Dolores González-Ripoll. *Trinidad: La Otra Llave de América – Descripción de la Isla de Trinidad por Cosme de Churruca y la Expedición del Atlas da la América Septentrional (1792/1810)*

Ottley, Carlton Robert. *The Story of Port of Spain from the Earliest Times to the Present*. Diego Martin, Trinidad: Crusoe Publications, 1977

Index

A

Abercromby, Sir Ralph, xiv, xv
Abolition of slavery (1838), xiv, 15, 35
Acanne, Maurice, 45
Agostini, Joseph Léon, 67
All Saints Church, 59
Ambard, Lucien F., 65
Anderson, Marion, 25
Anstey, Bishop Arthur, 63
Anthony C. Lewis Associates, 30
Archbishop's House, 66
Atwell, Winifred, 25

B

Bandstand, 25
Bath, Jonas Mohammed, 87
Belmont Hill, 74
Black Power protests (1970), 25
Boissière, Charles, 60
Boland, Frank, 73
Boos, Karl George, 51
Borde, Hippolyte, 9
Borde, Pierre Gustave, 6
Botanic Gardens, 71–2
BP Headquarters, 54–5
Bradshaw, Leslie, 84
Brian Lara Promenade, 1–4
Briar's End, 77–8
Bridgens, Richard, 25
Brinsley, Hubert, 14–15, 39
Brown, George (architect)
    Archbishop's House, 66
    Hayes Court, 63
    Jenny's, 51
    Milles Fleurs, 64
    Simpson House, 53
    St Ann's Church of Scotland, 48
    Union Club, 2
Bullbrook, John, 58

C

Cabildo Building, 37–8
Camps-Campins, Adrian, 77
Cathedrals
    Cathedral of the Immaculate Conception, 1–2, 6–7
    Trinity Cathedral, 28–9
Cazabon, Michel Jean, 58
Cedula of Population (1783), xii, xiv–xv, 49, 52
Centenary Hall, St Joseph's Convent, 42–3
Chacón, Governor Don José María, xv, 19, 23
Chantrey, Sir Francis Legatt, 29
Charlotte Street, 3
    Cathedral of the Immaculate Conception, 6
    St Ann's Church of Scotland, 48
Churches *see also* Cathedrals
    All Saints Church, 59
    Church of the Holy Rosary, 40
    Church of the Immaculate Conception, xv
    Greyfriars Church, 35
    Hanover Methodist Church, 35
    Holy Trinity Church, xv
    St Ann's Church of Scotland, 48
    St Patrick's Church, 50
Churruca, Don Cosme Damian de, 19
Cinemas
    Former Roxy Cinema, 78
    Metro cinema, 39–40
Cipriani, Captain Arthur Andrew, xv, 2, 13, 27

Cipriani, Michael (Mikey), 83
Cipriani Statue, 2, 13
City Gate, 9, 11–12
City Hall, 31
City Museum of Port of Spain, xii, xiv, 5
Collins, Tookie, 54
Columbus Square, 9
Colón, Cristóbal, xii
Colonial Bank, 2
Colonial Life Building, 17
Cricket ground, 76–7

D

Dowling, Archbishop, 66
Drinking trough, 22
Duke Street, 4
Duncan Street, 4
Duprey, Cyril, 17

E

Eastern Main Road, 22
Ecclesiastical Ordinance (1844), xv
Electricity, establishment of, xv, 54
Elizabeth Street, 77–8
Elliot, Governor Charles, 15
Emancipation of slaves, 15
Eric Williams Financial Complex, xv, 2, 15–16

F

Fernandes, J. B., 89
Flood, Archbishop Patrick, 66
Foon, Pat Chu, 86
Forts
    Fort Chacón, xiv, 19
    Fort George, 87
    Fort Picton, 20
    Fort San Andrés, xii, xiv, 5
Frederick Street
    Cabildo Building, 37

Cipriani Statue, 2, 13
Greyfriars Church, 35
National Museum and Art Gallery, 58
Port of Spain State Prison, 46
War Memorial Park, 58

G

General Hospital, 47
George Street, 6
Gillies, Robert, 68
Gingerbread House, 60
Globe cinema, 15, 39–40
Gordon, Governor Sir Arthur, 15
Gordon, William Gordon, 56, 59
Gordon Street, 47
Graf, Leonard, 45
Grant, Sir Lewis, 15
Great Fire (1808), xiv, 18
Greyfriars Church, 35

H

Hahn, Daniel Mienerts (architect)
    National Museum and Art Gallery, 58
    Queen's Royal College, 62–3
    The Red House, 25, 27
Haji Gokool Meah Memorial Masjid, 81
Hall of Justice, 30
Hanover Methodist Church, 35
Harris, Governor Lord, 15, 22, 25, 32, 73
Harris, Lady Sarah, 29
Hasley Crawford Stadium, 85–6
Hayes, Bishop Thomas, 63
Hayes Court, 63
Henderson, Robert, 67
Heritage Library, 32, 33
Hernández, José María, 40
Hill, Governor Sir George Fitzgerald, 15, 71
Hindu temple, 80
Hislop, Governor Sir Thomas, 74, 87
Hochoy, Governor-General Sir Solomon, 71–2, 75

Hollow, The, 73
Holy Ghost Fathers, 44
Holy Trinity Church, xv
Hospice of St Vincent de Paul, L', 21
Humphrey, William Pettigrew, 65

I

Ice House, 2
Independence (1962), xv, 16, 25, 75
Independence Square, 1–4
Irving, Governor Sir Henry Turner, 70

J

Jamaat al Muslimeen, 26, 36
James, C. L. R., 63
Jean Pierre Sports Complex, 85–6
Jeffers, Audrey, 77–8
Jeffers, Henry Israel, 77
Jenny's, 51

K

Keate, Governor William, 15
Keate Street, 58
Kennedy, Alexander, 35
Kent Street, 42
Killarney (Stollmeyer's Castle), 68–9
King Street, 4
Kingsley, Charles, 72
Knowsley, 56
Knox, William George, 32
Knox Street
    Hall of Justice, 30
    Old Library Building, 32

L

'Ladies of St Joseph,' 42
Laird, Colin (architect)
    Brian Lara Promenade, 1
    National Library, 33
    Queen's Hall, 75

Land reclamation, 9
Lange, Eugène, 44
Lapeyrouse Cemetery, 49
Léotaud, Dr Antoine, 57
Lewis, Anthony, 45
L'Hospice of St Vincent de Paul, 21
Lighthouse, 8
Lockhart, David, 71

M

MacLeod, Governor Sir Henry, xv, 15, 25
'Magnificent Seven' buildings, 61–9
Maraval Road, 61–9
Masonic Lodge, 18
Matouk, George, 64
Mckenzie, Pointz, 65
Meah, Gokool, 39–40
Menuhin, Yehudi, 40
Metro Cinema, 39–40
Milles Fleurs, 64
Minshall, Peter, 63
Morris, Ken, 27, 80
Mosque, 81
Munro, Governor Sir William, 46, 74
Museums
    City Museum of Port of Spain, xii, xiv, 5
    Museum of the Trinidad and Tobago Police Service, 36
    National Museum and Art Gallery, 57–8

N

Naipaul, V. S., 63, 68
National Library, 33
National Museum and Art Gallery, 57–8
Nelson Street, 3, 6
Newel-Lewis, John (architect)
    designs the Paschim Kaashi Mandir, 80
    on the Gingerbread House, 60
    on Queen's Royal College, 63
    on Roomor, 65
    on Whitehall, 68

Nicholas Tower, 2
Nti, Kofi, 87

O

Observatory Street, 21
Old Fire Brigade Building, 34
Old Library Building, 32
Old Police Headquarters, 36

P

Pantin, Anthony, 7
Parks
    Queen's Park Savannah, 52–3
    War Memorial Park, 58
Paschim Kaashi Mandir, 80
Pembroke Street, 45
People's National Movement (PNM), 25
Philip, Michel Maxwell, 49
Philip Street, 49
Picton, Sir Thomas, 20
Police Commissioner's House, 79
Population, xii, xiv–xv, 49, 52
Port of Spain General Hospital, 47
Port of Spain Lighthouse, 8
Port of Spain State Prison, 46
Prada, Dr Enrique, 64
President's House, 70–1
Public Transport Service Corporation, 12

Q

Queen's Hall, 75
Queen's Park Hotel, 54–5
Queen's Park Oval, 76–7
Queen's Park Savannah, 52–3
Queen's Royal College, xv, 25, 61–3

R

Railway, introduction of, xv
Railway Headquarters Building, 11–12

Rawle, Bishop Richard, 29
Red House, xv, 25–7
Reinagle, Philip, 28
Religious 'war,' xiv–xv
Robeson, Paul, 25
Roodal, Timothy, 65, 78
Roomor, 65
Roume de St Laurent, Philippe-Rose, xii, xiv, 5, 88
Roxy Cinema (former), 78

S

Sackville Street, 37
Salvatori, Joseph, 64
Samuels, Lewis, 47
Schools
    Queen's Royal College, xv, 25, 61–3
    St George's College, 44
    St Joseph's Convent, xv, 42–3
    St Mary's College, xv, 44–5
Sedeño, Antonio, 83
Simpson House, 53
Slavery
    abolition of (1838), xiv, 15, 35
    Trinidad Anti-Slavery Society, 35
South Quay, 9
Spaccapietra, Archbishop Vincent, 21
St Ann's Church of Scotland, 48
St Ann's Road, 58
St George's College, 44
St James Barracks, 79
St James Medical Complex, 82
St Joseph's Convent, xv, 42–3
St Mary's College, xv, 44–5
St Patrick's Church, 50
St Vincent Street, 35
    Colonial Life Building, 17
    Red House, 26
State Prison, 46
Stollmeyer's Castle (Killarney), 68–9
Sweet Briar Road, 77–8

T

Tamarind Square, 6
Treasury Building, 2, 14–15
Trinidad All Steel Percussion Orchestra (TASPO), 40
Trinidad Anti-Slavery Society, 35
Trinidad Country Club, 88–9
Trinidad Government Railway, xv, 11–12
Trinidad Hilton, 74
Trinidad Labour Party, 13
Trinidad Workingman's Association, 13
Trinity Cathedral, 28–9
Tripp, Edgar, xv
Turnbull, Gregor, 25

U

Union Club, 2
United Brothers Masonic Lodge, 18

V

Verteuil, Sir Louis de, 27
Victoria Avenue, 53

W

War Memorial Park, 58
Warner, Charles William, 71–2
Warner, Sir Pelham, 76
Water Riots (1903), 25
Waterfront, The, 9
Wellington Terrace, 58
Whitehall, 67–8
Williams, Dr Eric, 13, 16, 25, 63, 75
Woodbrook (Mucurapo) Cemetery, 83–4
Woodford, Governor Sir Ralph, 6–7, 23, 28, 29, 52, 71–2, 74, 89
Woodford Square, 23–5